STOICISM

STOICISM AND WISDOM FOR LEADERS

AUTHOR'S NAME:

Caterina Melians

Table of contents

STOICISM

STOICISM AND WISDOM FOR LEADERS; LEARN SELF-CONTROL AND HOW TO BE STRONGER USING MODERN CONCEPTS FOR MANAGERS

INTRODUCTION AND PRINCIPLES

Prologue to Stoicism

Stoicism underpins you to carry on with your best life. It resembles antiquated self-help, which has been attempted and confirmed for ages is as yet related today. Rehearsing Stoicism slopes to create a wide range of commonsense impacts (for example, diminishes negative emotions, builds positive emotions, improves execution, and advances life satisfaction), and it's anything but difficult to learn.

Stoicism doesn't require ruminating over your head for an hour a multi-day or learning an altogether extraordinary philosophical language. It was intentionally made to be reasonable, tremendous, and helpful. It offers straightforward procedures for more prominent tranquility and better living.

Stoic philosophy can change your mindset, increment your gladness, and give you more control over your life. You can, in any case, be content in any event, when things don't go how you need them. While we can't generally have control over the events in our lives, we can control how we approach them. It's having a renaissance right now with specialists, competitors, and government officials too. It's become a super-hotly debated issue.

Stoicism, don't get associated with authenticity, have dynamic coordinated efforts with your accomplices to bring them up, perform work relentlessly and for the higher extraordinary, and see what's in and out of your control — don't allow things to out of your control impact your joy. While confusing things happen, breathe in, see your inclination and the clarification behind it, and let it pass. You can't put everything in order in any case. All you could control is your reaction, and all that you can do is embody the goodness and worth all you have, which is something I'm certain we'll all find savor the experience of.

A short summation and definition of this particular school of Hellenistic perspective: Stoicism was built up by Zeno of Citium in the mid-third century BC in Athens. Nonetheless, was extensively bored by any similarity to Epictetus, Seneca, and Marcus Aurelius. The perspective proclaims that greatness, (for instance, insightfulness) is euphoria and judgment should be established on lead, rather than words. That we don't control and can't rely upon external events, just ourselves and our reactions.

Stoicism has just two or three central exercises. It chooses to assist us in remembering how unusual the world can be. How short our preview of life is. Bit by bit directions to be steady and trustworthy, and answerable for yourself, in conclusion, the wellspring of our failure lies in our rash dependence on our reflexive resources rather than justification.

Stoicism doesn't worry about jumbled theories about the world, yet with helping us vanquish harming emotions and follow up on what can be followed up on. It's worked for action, not ceaseless conversation.

It had three head pioneers. Marcus Aurelius, the leader of the Roman Empire, the most powerful man on earth, plunked during each opportunity to stay in contact with himself notes about limitation, compassion, and lowliness. Epictetus drove forward through the aversions of subjection to build up his one of a kind school where he indicated countless Rome's most commended characters. Seneca, when Nero turned on him and mentioned his suicide, could consider simply enhancing his loved one and buddies.

It isn't only those three—Stoicism that has been practiced by rulers, presidents, pros, researchers, and business visionaries. Both chronicled, and current men show Stoicism philosophy as a lifestyle.

The Prussian King, the individual of Frederick the Great, was said to ride with created by the Stoics in his saddlebags since they could, in his words, "bolster you in the episode." Meanwhile, Montaigne, the administrative authority and essayist, had a line from Epictetus cut into the pole over the assessment in which he contributed a huge segment of his vitality.

The setting up fathers were moreover energized by perspective. George Washington was familiar with Stoicism by his neighbors at age seventeen, and a brief timeframe later, performed Cato to awaken his men in that dull winter at Valley Forge. At the same time, Thomas Jefferson had a copy of Seneca on his end table when he kicked the can.

The business expert Adam Smith's theories on the interconnectedness of the world—private endeavor—were through and through affected by the Stoicism that he thought about as an understudy, under an instructor who had deciphered Marcus Aurelius' works.

The political researcher, John Stuart Mill, made out of Marcus Aurelius and Stoicism in his acclaimed treatise On Liberty, calling it "the most raised good aftereffect of the old character."

Stoicism shifts from most existing schools in one huge sense: its inspiration is rational application. It's not an only academic undertaking.

MAIN FUNDAMENTAL OF STOICISM

Step by step instructions to apply the fundamental principles in your own life

At the core of being human is the quest for an upbeat, satisfying life. We as a whole plan to carry on with real existence; we can feel extraordinary about recollecting.

That is the explanation I have such a friendship for Stoicism, an old philosophy that existed most noticeably all through the Roman and Greek times and included masterminds, for example, Marcus Aurelius and Seneca.

As of late, Stoicism has encountered a huge resurgence, fundamentally with agents who value its handy principles.

Stoicism is worried about two things:

1. Happiness

2. Potential

Those are the two things we're all looking for regardless of anything else. We need to carry on with a cheerful life and comprehend our maximum capacity. W for a moment to think about that: If you transformed into all that you arranged, you could ever be and found sprightliness all the while, what else would be left?

Here are some Stoic principles to take advantage of for an additionally fulfilling life:

Time is your most significant resource

We know consistently that our time is limited. In any case, how that the more noteworthy piece of us live is restricting that. We burn through quite a while at occupations we despise, stay with individuals we're not happy to be with, and generally recognize conditions that don't cause us to feel enchanted.

Remind yourself ordinarily that time is your most significant resource. You have so long to live, so attempt relentlessly to live to such an extent that will leave you with no apprehensions.

Apply what you understand

These days, it's anything but difficult to exhaust immense measures of data and get learning. Regardless, there's alongside no association between's get-together learning and genuine achievement.

You have to try to apply what you understand adequately. Not the only thing that is in any way important, clearly, yet when you read a book or get the hang of something that improves your craft, take cautious notes and make a game plan for applying that newfound data.

If you apply this principle, over and over, it will wind up being a bit of you. That is the point at which you advantage from the data.

Be thankful for what you have.

The advantages of thankfulness are by and upheld by look into. However, Marcus Aurelius and various Stoics talked about its capacity ages before us. Continuously should be appreciative of whatever you have. The thing isn't to care for all you have or that you won't get more, but since of the adjustment in the mindset that appreciation makes. Appreciation swings the mind from "I need," "I need a greater amount of" and "I wish I had" to "I'm so merry I have," "I'm grateful I'm" and "I'm cheerful I could."

The effort basic to change this is immaterial, yet the distinction by how you feel after some time is incredible.

Be accessible

The capacity to inconspicuously be with yourself, smoothly present and mindful of what's going on around you, is a sign you have locked in on the idea of your mind.

Be that as it may, the cool thing is, you can start practicing this now with no establishment or planning at all. Stop for a moment to be with yourself watchfully. hatNotice the feeling of breath on your lips, the climbing of your chest, sensations in the body, and any unmistakable encounters around you, for instance, passing cars or splendid light.

To be at the time is a powerful encounter loaded with benefits. Exploit it

Do whatever it takes not to scan for satisfaction in the material.

Over the top authenticity is one more sign of what I call "the void"– it's a delayed consequence of the inclination that something is missing inside us, something we continue loading up with material things.

The thing is, the likelihood that material things satisfy us was made by advancement people endeavoring to sell more things. It's not founded on any substantial information or logical research. Without a doubt, it feels extraordinary when we go from not having enough to having the alternative to bear the cost of the expense of things we've never asserted. However, that is a brief kind of enjoyment that can scarcely be seen as certifiable satisfaction.

The mind is your capacity.

Something that has helped Stoicism resurge in appreciation is that it shares much for all intents and purpose with the philosophy that frequently accompanies mindfulness meditation.

This principle has an inseparable tie to self-mindfulness, and understanding that by controlling your mind, you're prepared to live a progressively cheerful, progressively quiet life.

What you should control is your own one of a kind mind. You can work to impact outside conditions. However, that is an exertion that is clashing, the most ideal situation. By figuring out how to ace the mind, you'll find your life and comprehend a power unquestionably more noticeable than anything outside yourself.

Recall your why

At the point when you're moving in the direction of a major objective, making sense of you're the reason that is, the explanation you need what you're advancing towards is one of the fundamental things of all.

Not as much since it motivates you when things are acceptable; however, it's more since realizing why you're buckling down aids you hold tight when things turn out badly.

Consider how you burn through your effort.

On some arbitrary day, what measure of time do you spend towards what is significant most to you? Burning through the effort with your family? Tackling your strength? Managing yourself?

Do you experience hours utilizing web-based life? Tattle destinations? Arbitrarily glancing through Reddit until you comprehend an hour has passed by, and you've done nothing gainful?

High-achievers will, as a rule, be unfathomable at sorting out what is generally crucial to them, so consider what you burn through your effort doing and make the basic changes to comprehend the existence you had constantly needed.

See that all that we experience begins from inside.

It's barely noticeable that all that we experience occurs in the space between our ears: outrage, distress, satisfaction, harmony, overthinking, stress, dread, re-thinking, lament, certainty, and everything in the middle.
Our emotions depict our encounters. What's more, it's in the mind that we pick what emotions to react with established on those encounters.

See that all that we experience makes from inside, and you'll comprehend that you have fundamentally control on your thought over how you feel on a regular premise.

Figure out how to manage the area of your emotions, and you'll make sense of how to ace a major piece of satisfaction.

Change your perspective on disillusionment.

It's entirely expected to believe the powerlessness to be negative. You've taken a stab at something, and it wasn't adequate. Regardless, your last strategy to be to transform into the perfect variation of yourself (and afterward utilizing that likelihood to serve others).

In the event that you investigate things thusly, every mistake transforms into a profitable open entryway for self-improvement, a chance to use as a venturing stone to for all intents and purposes unavoidable accomplishment.

Have a good example to gauge your character

It's difficult to quantify your advancement as a person without anything to gauge it against. Similarly, it's terrible to quantify yourself against individuals who are not good idealistic examples.

You have to find someone that motivated you in light of their tremendous character, which means the characteristics you find generally required. When you've seen somebody you can aim as like, you'll have a benchmark you can reliably use to check your advancement.

5 Stoic Principles for Modern Living

The a lot of thought into how life should be lived, from Aristotle to Socrates to Plato, yet one of their most valuable perspectives stays misinterpreted by a large portion of the people: Stoicism. Notwithstanding Stoicism's undeserved reputation for being synonymous with aloofness, it can provoke an incomprehensibly satisfying lifestyle. Stoicism is an old perspective that can be cleaned by anyone to fabricate their euphoria; various thoughts you may consider as now practice in your step by step participation.

Stoicism is, at its root, a perspective for constraining the negative emotions throughout your life and intensifying your gratefulness and bliss; it consolidates care practices and worth based living. Stoicism is a gadget to upgrade your human experience, both inside and remotely. Right now, share a bit of the manner in which those Stoics think by explaining the importance behind a few their most notable pro's announcements. By solidifying a piece of their perspectives into our regular day to day existences, I acknowledge we'll find more satisfaction in our step by step commitments and respond even more flexibly to issues and troubles that develop.

Rule 1: You can't change things outside of your control, yet you can change your mood.

A key section of Stoicism is practicing care. See the events throughout your life that you do and don't have direction over. In the event that you become disillusioned with conditions outside of your control, you are wasting imperativeness and developing a negative feeling. A Buddhist story best frameworks the stoic daily schedule with respect to protecting your mind from conditions out of your control. The foe in the story is Mara, an enemy of the Buddha. Mara thought about the Buddha's powers and attempted to pulverize him, so he sent an amazing outfitted power. Mara instructed the troopers to hurl flaring rocks at the Buddha, yet when they drew near to him, they went to blooms and fell. Buddha's enemy by then prepared the military to shoot jolts at the Buddha, anyway again, the jolts advanced toward turning out to bloom once they gravitated toward the Buddha's circle. There was nothing Mara could do to hurt the Buddha in light of the fact that the Buddha had aced the capacity to shield his happiness from outside events. I draw equal the stones and dashes to negative thoughts about open-air conditions. You can't change these events; you can change your mood towards them. Through this affirmation, our mind can end up immune. Since we can control our mindsets and reactions, we can very well never be conversely affected by outside events.

Rule 2: Don't fall prey to current society's materialistic nature.

Our consumerist society seems to make more need than it fulfills. These results in everyone are remaining mindful of the Jones' — yet it's questionable that even the Jones' are happy. Our steady prologue to media and advancing keeps us requiring and seeing better out there — we spend our merited money on the latest winning style, convinced it will leave us fulfilled until structure 2.0 diverts out one year from now. In the event that we attempt to unnecessary, our aching reduces, and we become progressively content with what we have, which conveys us to the accompanying explanation.

Rule 3: Picture existence without the people and resources you have to esteem them.

We've seen now that requiring more prompts frustration — so how might we find satisfaction? The key lies in appreciation. We should respect all that we have and find a rapture in it. We live in a staggering time of history with straightforward access to necessities and advancement that gives a lifestyle that was unforeseeable just two or three pages back. Instead of esteeming this, we belittle it. The stoic practice is to imagine that you lost a few your huge possessions. It may sound disheartening from the outset; notwithstanding, by imagining these setbacks, we come to recognize what we have more. It's fundamental that we not put an abundance of need on the things we have either — for they may not generally be there. Being Stoic techniques finding delight through whatever you do have — if you place a highlight on an outside thing and it is evacuated, the stoic should not be upset yet rather grateful they had the thing regardless. Everything is gotten from the universe. Mass voyages all over. In any case, goodness remains, and in that falsehoods satisfaction.

Rule 4: Be really light-footed in the aggregate of your joint efforts.

We presently understand that euphoria starts from inside and from recognizing everything around us — despite something as clear as living at a point in time where we can buy separated water for $1.00 from a treat machine near 100 feet from us (We really disparage things now and again). Since, with the stoic viewpoint, our satisfaction can end up liberated from various factors, we ought to be happy all the time as stoics since we don't need anything over human experience. In case we needed more, we could empower ourselves to be disappointed. This doesn't suggest that Stoics can't value the better things throughout everyday life — it just methods we shouldn't think of them as fundamental for our satisfaction. Simply offering goodness to the world through helping people and pushing society — something we each can do once per day — can make us fulfilled.

Rule 5: Practicing your characteristics beats addressing them.

Stoic perspective requires an incredible course of action of good commitment. It isn't such a lot that you should be frantically hard on yourself, yet you should understand that every decision that you make for the day contains a moral estimation. Stoicism must be bored in the event that you have to affect the world in a predominant manner. Ask yourself, for the most part, "What's the perfect method to act right now?" should like to choose choices reliant on your characteristics to growth.

THE CORE VIRTUES OF STOICISM

Practical wisdom –

This suggests having the option to investigate tangled conditions in an intelligent, coherent, and quiet way.

Instead of endeavoring to envision an ideal society, Stoics deal with the world, all things considered. They additionally centered on little things and avoided vanity.

Moderation –

Another word for this is self-discipline. This implies practicing self-restriction and control in all aspects of your life.

A couple of Stoics accepted that nourishment was basically the perfect way to deal with test your self-control and moderation. Nourishment gets showed to us consistently. It's vital forever, however, not for delight. Stoics had faith in eating to live, not living to eat.

Fortitude –

Stoics allude to this as the spine. They didn't simply have confidence in mental strength in remarkable conditions. They put confidence in going up against your ordinary difficulties with clearness and genuineness.

Equity –

Treating others with reasonableness, in any event, when they have committed an error.

Stoics accepted that failure is visit, yet that lament is moronic. They additionally encouraged individuals to live each day as though it were their last.

OTHER STOIC VIRTUES

The Stoics were people who sought after a pragmatic anyway morally constructive method for continuing with, a perspective of life made by Hellenistic Greeks and vivaciously got a handle on by the Romans. The Stoic perspective had a significant interest to Christian researchers of the mid-twentieth century, which echoes in our own propelled culture.

"I acknowledge that [Stoicism] addresses a method for looking world and the rational issues of life which have still an invariable excitement for mankind, and an enduring force of inspiration. I will move toward it, thusly, perhaps as an advisor over as a philosopher or history specialist... I will just endeavor splendidly well to make sound its incredible central gauges and the basically overpowering interest which they made to such an enormous number of the best characters of times long past." Knapp 1926

Stoics: From Greek to Roman Philosophy

The masterminds who sought after Aristotle (384-322 BC) were known as the Peripatetics, named for their walking around the halls of the Athenian Lyceum. The Stoics, on the other hand, were named for the Athenian Stoa Poikile or "painted yard," where one of the creators of the Stoic perspective, Zeno of Citium (in Cyprus) (344-262 BC), trained. While the Greeks may have developed considering Stoicism from the past strategies for reasoning, we have areas of their exercises. Their perspective is consistently isolated into three sections, basis, material science, and ethics.

Various Romans got the perspective as a lifestyle or claim to fame of living (téchnê peri tón bion in the old Greek)- - as it was proposed by the Greeks- - and it is from the all-out records of superb period Romans, especially crafted by Seneca (4 BC-65 AD), Epictetus (c. 55-135) and Marcus Aurelius (121-180) that we increment most by far of our information about the ethical game plan of the principal Stoics.

Stoic Principles

Today, Stoic measures have found their way into recognized notable knowledge, as goals to which we should seek after - as in the Serenity Prayer of Twelve Step programs.

Coming up next are eight of the fundamental thoughts in the domain of ethics that were held by the Stoic researchers.

- Nature - Nature is rational.

- Law of Reason - The universe is spoken to by the law of clarification. Man can't escape from its constant power, yet he can, phenomenally, cling to the law deliberately.

- Virtue - An actual existence drove by adaptable nature is judicious.

- Wisdom - Wisdom is the root of morals. From it springs the cardinal excellencies: getting, fearlessness, circumspection, and value.

- Apatheia - Since excitement is nonsensical, and life should be sought after as a battle against it. The outrageous tendency should be avoided.

- Pleasure - Pleasure isn't extraordinary. (Nor is it dreadful. It is only commendable in case it doesn't interfere with our main goal for morals.)

- Evil - Poverty, illness, and passing are not naughty.

- Duty - Virtue should be searched for, not for euphoria, yet the commitment.

MINDFULNESS

Stoic mindfulness comes down to recognizing what is in our control, and that which isn't. Stay present, and you will get mindful of those things that are out of our control. This makes it simpler to concentrate on actions that are probably going to have positive results.

The guarantee of stoicism is astonishing: Not just will you generally settle on the choices that are directly for you, your family, and the network, yet you will do as such while carrying on with a peaceful life in absolute offset with yourself and the world.

It sounds unrealistic. Particularly in the event that you've been lying perspiring in the totally dark evening having battled throughout the previous 4 hours to nod off with seething cataclysmic doomsday thoughts spinning out of control as wild steeds in your mind.

The most disappointing thing about stoicism is beginning, this book clarifies why and afterward an answer for how to begin.

The order of significant worth judgment

One of the main stoic controls you will experience is the Discipline of "significant worth judgment" — or "Recognition." This order guarantees — in the event that you can pull it off — that you can change the manner in which you feel about anything.

The substance of significant worth judgment is depicted to Choose not to be hurt — and you won't feel hurt. Try not to feel hurt, and you haven't been.

In its pith, on the off chance that you can decide not to be hurt by some occasion — for example, your manager shouting at you, the way that it's coming down on your grill night, the way that the trains are late and now you're running late for a significant gathering and so on — at that point you won't be hurt and subsequently can respond increasingly normal to the occasion. This means it isn't occasioned themselves that damage us, yet our worth judgment about that occasion that damages us. At the end of the day, the worth we allocate to some occasion that causes us to hurt. In the event that we can simply quit doing that, at that point, we won't ever be hurt by anything!

The issue with applying this principle is that too numerous individuals the damage of an occasion (someone said something negative, something terrible happened and so on) is that the occasion and the mark "awful," "negative," appear to follow consequently with the occasion. You experience something, and you understand it's awful; you respond sincerely to it.

The three phases of understanding

As indicated by the stoic philosophy, the way toward encountering an occasion and responding to it really has three phases:

1. Primary portrayal: We experience an occasion and structure our essential portrayal of that occasion. For example, what is this occasion? For example, somebody fell on their bicycle, and someone challenges our knowledge; someone is shouting at us. Just the occasion that really occurred as a general rule and not what it "signifies" to us. This is only the unadulterated interpretation of tangible information to a portrayal that the mind can comprehend and work with.

2. Value-judgment: We dole out an incentive for this essential portrayal. For example, it's awful, it's acceptable, and it's charming, it's nonpartisan — for example what the occasion "signifies" to us, and we structure a thought regarding the proper behavior on occasion.

3. Assent: Finally, we settle on a choice about whether to go about as the worth judgment proposed we do. It is possible that we acknowledge it, or we dismiss it. Maybe the proposal: "We should choke our chief" gets dismissed, however, "how about we shout at her" strength goes as an astounding method to respond.

The decision that alludes to lies in the consent arrangement. The issue today is that we experience these three phases so blazingly quick that we don't understand that there's a decision.

This shows an issue to the stoic devotee as the stoic mind-tricks applies just at the worth judgment arrange:

… consistently to characterize whatever it is that we see — to follow it's a blueprint — so we can perceive what it truly is: its substance. Stripped uncovered. In general. Unmodified. What's more, to call it by its name.

You can just apply this stunt directly after the essential portrayal has materialized. In any case, if your mind runs arrange 1–3 on autopilot, how might you deactivate this autopilot?

Tangible preparing

One stage wasn't referenced in the above procedure of encountering an occasion. That is the progression directly before the essential portrayal. The progression that goes before that may be abridged as "Sensoric input." This is where someone addresses us, or we witness something with our eyes, etc. Any sort of sensoric input that leads us to frame an essential portrayal of some occasion. This sensoric input is the genuine target portrayal of what occurred (accepting our tangible organs are normal). With no connection of significant worth. This is the crude tactile information.

For reasons unknown, any sort of tactile information experiences a similar three-phase process: Primary portrayal, Value-judgment, and Assent. For example, You see someone fall on their bicycle:

The essential portrayal lets you know: Somebody fell on their bicycle.

Worth judgment in a split second responds: Holy crap, I should run there and check whether the individual is alright.

Consent: Ok, go do it.

Or then again: Your manager shouts at you for not joining the correct report to an email

The essential portrayal lets you know: Your supervisor hollers at you for not joining the correct record to an email.

Worth judgment in a split second responds: He is testing my insight and believe I'm moronic. I better reveal to him that I'm not f***ing moronic.

Consent: Ok, go do it.

In the primary case, the tangible info is visual. In the second, sound-related. All tactile info is handled similarly.

Meditation and the tingle

You're presumably pondering at this point, why the title of this post is "stoicism and mindfulness meditation" when I haven't composed a solitary word about meditation as of not long ago. Well here goes (and this is the significant piece of this post in spite of the fact that it may initially appear to be silly):

In the event that you've attempted to ruminate, I ensure that you will have encountered a tingle while thinking. In the primary months of your meditation practice, you simply scratch it: "Good day's a tingle — how about we scratch it! I'll effectively escape this exhausting meditation!"

A decent meditation practice instructs you to let any tangible information, whether agony, tingles, and even thoughts, simply coast on by without responding to them. Regularly, on the off chance that you understand (a thought) that you neglected to purchase milk while ruminating, you don't surge out the entryway and get it for the basic explanation that you're as of now thinking and you can do it a short time later. Though tingles and torment you respond to consequently: Your leg nodding off: You move a bit. You sense and tingle: You scratch, and so on. It's on autopilot. You take care of business. You probably won't know that you did it.

When you understand that you shouldn't really scratch the tingle while pondering, you begin giving close consideration to what happens when you go from detecting the tingle to really scratching it. What's more, after numerous more hours reflecting and of seeming as though somebody with serious ticks battling the development of your own hand, you begin to acknowledge (and this is the significant part) where there's a physical sensation in your mind joined to the demonstration of distinguishing the tingle. What's more, if you can distinguish that, at that point, you can prevent your hand from moving by any stretch of the imagination! Truth be told, this precise point in time where you recognize the tingle is the place you get the essential portrayal, for example, the most unadulterated portrayal of what the occasion you're responding to is.

Also, you recognize what the enjoyment part is (yes, there are really interesting parts about a tingle)? On the off chance that you simply disregard the tingle, it leaves without anyone else. Henceforth similarly as the stoics anticipated: It's you and only you that append a negative an incentive to something. What's more, the main motivation behind why you scratch it, in any case, is on the grounds that you apply a worth judgment of "terrible."

Feel the pre-tingle sensation

On the off chance that you work on recognizing the physical sensation in your mind identified with distinguishing a tingle while reflecting, you can begin to feel a similar sensation when you're out on the town in reality. Next time your manager hollers at you, feel the equivalent pre-tingle sensation that emerges from the interaction and stops any action in that spot. Take a gander at this essential portrayal and apply the stoic mind-tricks to that so you can carry on reasonably and in an ideal manner.

So in case you're tingling to begin applying stoic philosophy in your life, I can enthusiastically suggest this little stunt, which is so basic it tingles: Just quit scratching the tingle.

Stoic Meditation Exercises

Here are the four Stoic meditation techniques it incorporates:

Examination of the Sage.

Envision the instance of the ideal Stoic smart man or woman, and how they would adjust to various challenges throughout everyday life. Endeavor to express their frames of mind, which you can recollect as short platitudes or precepts. Moreover, think about models, for instance, Socrates, Zeno, Epictetus, or Marcus Aurelius or other explicit genuine models from history, fiction, or your own life.

Examination of Death.

Intermittently think about your own mortality, seeing it impartially, and as both common and unavoidable. Each morning remind yourself that the day ahead could be your last; each night envisions seeing the day behind you as though it were your last. Endeavor to live grounded in the present moment, valuing the endowment of life as though you're a guest at a festival or supper, which you know will keep going for a limited timeframe.

Thought of the Whole.

Envision the whole world as though observed from high above, similar to the awesome creatures looking down from Mount Olympus. On the other hand, endeavor to envision the whole of the real world and your place inside things. Consider likewise the short existence of each and every material thing, and the short period of time that human life keeps going.

Premeditation of Adversity

Work on envisioning diverse "calamities" that could happen upon you, as though they're going on now, while keeping up Stoic objectivity and aloofness toward them, concentrating on the differentiation between what is up to you and what isn't, and permitting satisfactory time for your underlying emotions to subside normally. Think about how, as a Stoic sage would react to comparable events.

Attempting Stoic Meditations

Picture your place in the world.

The Hierocles' Circle is a Stoic visualization practice that causes you to consider how you fit into the terrific arrangement of things. Start by picturing yourself, by then envision your family and partners around you. Picture your associates, neighbors, and partners in the accompanying circle, your city in the accompanying and, definitely, the entirety of mankind, the entirety of Nature, and the entirety of the nearness.

- Take around 10 minutes to do the action. In the event that it energizes you focus, sits in a quiet spot, close your eyes, and take moderate, full breaths.

- The point is to welcome that things are interconnected. You're a bit of an interpersonal organization and, at last, connected to the entire universe.

Take a stab at envisioning extraordinary adversity.

A premeditation Malorum is a Stoic meditation wherein you envision losing something that is fundamental to you, similar to your movement or a companion or relative. Picture a negative circumstance in your mind just for two or three minutes or something like that. It sounds upsetting, yet the fact of the matter is to recognize temporariness, plan for blocks, consider the helpful things throughout your life, and defeat your sentiments of fear.

- Negative visualization can help fabricate mental quality in spite of uncontrollable deterrents. That infers when something horrendous happens, you may have a simpler time adapting in the event that you've quite recently envisioned it.

Peruse a step by step quote and think about its importance.

Consistently, investigate a short quote by a Stoic researcher. We should accept it on various events to yourself and think about its importance. Whether or not it was made more than 2,000 years back, consider how you could apply its significance to your own one of a kind life.

- You could look online for proclamations by scholars like Epictetus, Seneca, and Marcus Aurelius.

- You can likewise discover explanations, reflections, and various resources on astute online diaries.

Compose an intelligent journal section at the piece of the deal. At the piece of the deal, elucidate the troubles you went up against and the choices you made. Mull over a negative standard of conduct you attempted to improve. Consider how you could have chosen a prevalent choice or dealt with a circumstance in an unexpected way.

• For occurrence, you may communicate, "Today Sam was short with me. I started to state something back; however got myself before I lost my cool. I'm showing signs of improvement about not permitting others to get under my skin, yet at the same time, have some work to do."

WISDOM AND LESSON LEARNED FROM STOICISM

The old philosophy of Stoicism is fiercely well known right now. Long dead Stoic scholars, for example, Marcus Aurelius and Seneca the Younger have become top of the line creators. The self-help industry, which has rediscovered and repackaged Stoicism as a type of self-help philosophy.

This repackaging is halfway the motivation behind why Stoicism is one of the most misconstrued and mishandled philosophical schools.

Stoicism is regularly offered to us as a philosophy for "action," for occupied individuals who don't have the opportunity to think about over philosophical riddles about existence. Specifically citing Seneca the Younger, Marcus Aurelius and Epictetus outside of any relevant connection to the subject at hand would give anyone the solid impression that that is the situation.

Somehow or another "Stoicism," as it is lectured by numerous individuals of its new followers, is the new fallacy: a method for really maintaining a strategic distance from thought and hard reasoning. A "philosophy for action," just as being a logical inconsistency in wording, is one that underestimates things, that lays on given presumptions.

A System of Thought

Stoicism illuminates action in its moral pretense yet is unmistakably in excess of moral philosophy. The Stoic scholars of antiquated Greece built up a hypothesis of the universe, a material science, an arrangement of rationale, and a hypothesis of reality that the morals of Stoicism basically get from. The very premise of Stoicism is not to underestimate things however, to think about the very idea of our being.

Co-heads Marcus Aurelius and Lucius Verus. Marcus was accidentally one of the extraordinary popularisers of Stoicism, a philosophy that has antiquated Greek starting points. His own diaries, put something aside for children and inevitably distributed, are brimming with Stoic thoughts. The way that Marcus drew such a great amount of solidarity from Stoicism as both a military and state pioneer exhibits the power of philosophy. (source: Wikipedia)

At the core of Stoicism, as most different schools of philosophy, is the grasp of examination. Therefore their scholarly commitment to the old world was gigantic. A definitive exercise of Stoicism is this: to carry on with a satisfying life is to ask yourself troublesome inquiries about what it is to be a person. The Stoics prized reason for the exclusion of everything else, and reason requires discipline.

It is regularly said that philosophy is the endeavor to respond to the inquiry "by what means should I live?" To endeavor to address that question requires thinking of a sensible comprehension of the world and your connection to it.

It's not really about finding an "extreme truth," it's tied in with discovering traction to stroll with when such a significant number of others are slipping near.

Knowing yourself and your place on the planet will permit you to consider how you should live and ensure you satisfy the qualities that you set for yourself.

Meditation specialists frequently offer the accompanying guidance: in case no doubt about it to think for ten minutes per day, you ought to reflect for an hour daily.

This is valid for examination as well. On the off chance that you are too occupied to even think about contemplating life, you're diverting yourself from your life, and you have to consider more. As Marcus Aurelius expressed: "an incredible satisfaction relies on the nature of your thoughts." Like everything advantageous throughout everyday life, quality thoughts don't come simple.

This has help from the curve of Marcus Aurelius portrays the head during the Marcomannic Wars against Germanic brutes, 176–180 AD. Marcus is frequently delineated in the posture of offering pardon to vanquished foes. (source: Wikipedia)

Under the tutorship of Diognetus and Junius Rusticus, Marcus Aurelius grasped the plainness of the scholarly lifestyle. As a kid, he wore an "unpleasant" shroud and would rest on the floor. He composed that his mom showed him "strict devotion, straightforwardness in diet" and staying far from the "methods for the rich."

Marcus shared power for some time with Lucius Verus, his supportive sibling. The two acquired a domain at a pained time in its history. Immense relocations of individuals started to squeeze pressure on the Roman fringes, and Rome had gotten entangled in a few long wars with the Parthian Empire and a few Germanic clans in the north. These contentions went on for Marcus' whole rule.

He was successful in every one of the wars he battled. However, the cost of triumph was high: armies coming back from Parthia carried a plague with them that crushed the Empire's populace and may have executed his co-ruler.

Meditations

His own notes, which proceeded to be distributed as The Meditations of Marcus Aurelius, have a stamped despairing about them. The logician was a hesitant ruler, exhausted of contention, and looked for comfort in his own thoughts as Stoics accepted they should.

His works were expected to be private; thus, his thoughts are deprived of the rational setting from which they infer. Marcus was not framing any contentions or speculations and accordingly didn't have to reference the rationalists that preceded him in any profundity. He was just journaling his rational thoughts.

Romans During the Decadence, Thomas Couture, 1847. Marcus Aurelius was raised in an exceptionally well off family yet was raised to spurn the trappings of the outrageous abundance of Rome. His humility and balance made him a well-known sovereign. (source: Wikipedia)

Marcus is extremely regularly quoted outside of any relevant connection to the issue at hand. Concise, persuasive proclamations are scholarly low-quality nourishment. Marcus was thoroughly educated in Stoic philosophy, and as a real savant, the sovereign merits better.

His guide Fronto wrote to Marcus, "it is better never to have contacted the educating of philosophy… then to have tasted it externally, with the edge of the lips." The foreordained head accepted the mentor's recommendation and completely grasped the Stoic philosophy until his passing.

Marcus Aurelius' philosophy in ten citations

Beneath, I have taken a "best 10" of Marcus Aurelius quotes and set them with regards to Stoic philosophy. Going with each quote is a short development that will spread out the fundamental principles of Stoic philosophy in a cautious successive request. These developments will give you a superior clarification on how the quotes could assist you with examining life.

1. The solidarity of all things

"Everything is connected with each other, and this unity is consecrated."

The unity of the universe is an old thought in philosophy. This is designated "monism."

Monism is the conviction that there is eventually one substance that shows in a majority of appearances (like fire, water, earth, and tissue). Most Stoics accepted the one substance was God. Marcus stated: "there are one substance and one law, to be specific, basic explanation in all reasoning animals, and all fact is one if, as we accept, there is just a single way of flawlessness for all creatures who share a similar mind."

Since God is in all things and not isolated from us — there is no domain higher than nature, and God is all-invading in nature — one should act as per nature to be near God.

Eminent defenders of the possibility of monism incorporate Parmenides (c. 500 BC) and Baruch Spinoza (seventeenth century). Zeno of Elias, a supporter of Parmenides, endeavored to show the unity of things with his well-known conundrums.

2. Everything is foreordained

"Everything that happens occurs as it should, and in the event that you watch cautiously, you will see this as so."

In the event that the universe involves various parts of a celestial one, at that point, everything must be great. In the case of everything is great, at that point, everything can be no other way.

The Stoics accepted that all occasions are foreordained (this is classified "determinism" in philosophy) and that you have either no control or next to no control over conditions. Everything is fated. Numerous Stoics had faith in divination (fortune-telling) techniques, for example, soothsaying and parts (what could be compared to tarot cards) since everything, regardless of how apparently inconsequential, is interconnected in fate.

Some portion of the Column of Marcus Aurelius to recognize his triumph over the Germanic clans. On the privilege is portrayed "the marvel of downpour" (delineated as a sort of downpour god). At one phase of the war against the Quadi clan, the Roman soldiers were caught and had gotten depleted by a lack of hydration inferable from a dry spell. A gigantic tempest opened up and recharged Marcus' soldiers with the water adequate to retaliate and vanquish the Quadis. Stoics comprehend that nature is great and can't be changed. Everything, even apparently supernatural occasions, was foreordained.

3. You have power over your mind, yet not occasions.

"You have the power over your mind — not outside occasions. Understand this, and you will discover quality."

You will most likely be unable to change the course of occasions, yet you do, be that as it may, have control over your own thoughts and emotions. This is the way Stoicism is unequivocally connected with poise: things can go gravely, yet we can control our reaction. To just realize this is to discover mental quality. Mental quality is the thing that the Stoics are celebrated for. Catastrophe and life's good and bad times are met with quiet and nobility.

Marcus Aurelius lost, at any rate, two newborn child youngsters. In an unprecedented section of Meditations, he expressed: "One man supplicates: 'How I may not lose my little kid,' however you should implore: 'How I may not be hesitant to lose him.'"

The distinction between the Stoic and the regular man is right now; basic man implores that he is saved of adversity, the Stoic asks that he can discover the solidarity to acknowledge setback.

English government-funded schools encouraged Stoicism as a component of an old-style instruction, and it is generally thought answerable for the renowned British "firm upper lip" — a feeling of serenity in intense, even shocking, conditions.

4. The obstacle is the way

"The obstacle to action propels action. What disrupts the general flow turns into the way."

Since everything, as indicated by the Stoics, is resolved — "everything that happens occurs as it should" — you couldn't take care of the obstacles you may confront. Rather the mind can just discover an open door in the snag on the grounds that the mind is all that we really have control over.

The full quote is as per the following: "Our actions might be blocked. However, there can be no obstructing our aims or miens. Since we can oblige and adjust. The mind adjusts and changes over to its own motivations the obstruction to our acting. The hindrance to action progresses action. What disrupts the general flow turns into the way." (My accentuation).

Right now is a sort of speculative chemistry of fate: issues and missteps become brilliant exercises, catastrophes can become open doors for profound development.

5. There is no single truth we can know, just points of view

"All that we get is a point of view, not a reality. All that we see is a point of view, not reality."

The universe is great and genuine, yet we are nevertheless one piece of the entire, so in this manner can't completely realize that flawlessness and truth. Here Marcus is rehearsing "perspectivism," another old and ongoing theme in the philosophy that rejects that we can get to an extreme truth.

In contrast to "relativism," which sees no reality on the planet at all, perspectivism doesn't limit the possibility of truth. In any case, our comprehension of things is imperfect and socially interceded, such that we can't completely get to reality. Each feeling is a point of view that is to a more noteworthy or lesser degree near reality, however not the ideal truth.

6. There is no, and there can be no, reliable person

"… the dependable man doesn't exist."

Since there are just points of view that are pretty much obvious (and never completely valid), there can be no conclusive judgment. Stoicism doesn't guarantee impeccable information. In the event that there is no more significant position authority than reason and nature is administered by reason, at that point, no man can have trustworthiness, not by any means the Roman sovereign himself.

This comes down to the contrast among insight and wisdom: the genuinely shrewd man knows the points of confinement of his knowledge.

Seneca the Younger was Nero's guide and political consultant. Sometime down the road, Nero turned on him and requested that he end his own life.

7. Be righteous in real life, not in principle

"Burn through no additional time contending what a decent man ought to be. Be one."

The scholar ruler is embracing "prudence morals," the possibility that great lead radiates from great character. There are two other major moral formulae: "consequentialist" morals: the hypothesis that the best actions are those with the best results, and "deontological" — or obligation — morals: that ideals live just in the demonstration itself, not the outcomes of the demonstration.

aitThe major difference between the two is that the previous would permit you to tell an "innocent embellishment" on the off chance that you realized that great would happen to it, the last position would contend that all untruths are characteristically awful and you ought not to lie paying little mind to the results.

Though consequentialism is guided by anticipated results and deontological morals by principles, they are defective since they depend on our flawed points of view. Excellence morals depend not on principles yet on the character. The Stoic rationalist Epictetus contended that if you somehow managed to live as per nature, you would act fittingly; there would be no compelling reason to either figure the results of your actions or learn rules to direct them.

8. You are what you think

"The things you consider decide the nature of your mind. Your spirit assumes the shade of your thoughts."

On the off chance that morals lie in highminded character, at that point, how we act at last comes down to thought and reason.

Emotions for the Stoics are decisions and along these lines subjective. Covetousness, for instance, is a bogus judgment about the inborn estimation of cash or assets. Since the method for the Stoic is to live as per nature, the reason must be prized regardless of anything else, since the universe is administered by the laws of reason.

9. The endless importance of our lives

"What we do in life swells in forever."

So far, we've discovered that Marcus Aurelius and the Stoics accepted that the universe is God: it is great, genuine and everlasting (what is impeccable must be interminable).

Individuals regularly bring out the tremendousness of the universe to show how minor and unimportant our lives are: only a bit of residue in a monstrous universe with a long life expectancy that might be valid. In any case, these individuals are limiting boundlessness. In a vast universe, our thoughts and actions take on a gigantic centrality since they are a piece of an unending chain.

10. The examination will give you a glad life

"A mind-blowing bliss relies on the nature of your thoughts."

We ought not to avoid the multifaceted nature of the world we live in or the intricacy of ourselves. On the off chance that we ponder, we also can be liberated from passionate unrest, profound exhaustion, and tangled reasoning.

It requires some investment and fortitude to think about. In the event that we are honored with the previous, we should grasp the last mentioned.

USE OF STOICISM TO LEARN SELF-CONTROL

Whether or not you're keen on Stoic perspective or should be stoic as it's characterized in the lexicon, endeavor to work on balance and mindfulness. Remember, you can control your actions and choices. However, most things are out of your hands and not worth your weight. Being a stoic doesn't mean you should be cold and difficult to reach, so think before you talk rather than not talking using any and all means. Notwithstanding endeavoring to be stoic in the step by step life, you can dive further into Stoic perspective by giving ordinary meditations and mirroring a shot philosophical explanations.

Building up a Stoic Mindset

Recognize what you can't change.

A couple of things, for instance, world events and catastrophic events, are outside your ability to control, and there's no use thumping yourself about something you can't change. Concentrate rather on things you can change, similar to your own choices and choices.

Think about a tennis coordinate. You can't control things like the capacity of your adversary, the mediator's calls, or how sporadic breeze impacts may impact the ball. Then again, you can pick the sum to practice before the game, to show up well-invigorated, and not stay up for the duration of the late evening celebrating before the match.

Try not to worry over others.

There's nothing amiss with conversing with people, however, take the necessary steps not to wander anxiously and aimlessly. You can't control others, so there's no motivation to be uncertain. You shouldn't feel like you have to adjust to others' models, principally on the off chance that it implies trading off your own one of kind morals.

Think before you talk and sincerely react.

Work on having restrictions and mindfulness dynamically. Being a stoic doesn't have anything to do with just not talking. It's logically fundamental to think before you talk, whether or not you're keen on philosophical Stoicism or should be stoic in the lexicon sense.

- For model, on the off chance that somebody affronts you, don't simply declare an angry affront back at them. Try not to associate with them in an enthusiastic fight, yet consider if there's any reality to their announcement and consider how you could better yourself.

- If you feel yourself getting resentful and can't concentrate on the circumstance's substances, endeavor to envision charming environment, sing a tune in your mind, or express a stoic mantra to yourself, for instance, "If it's not in my control, it's none of my anxiety."

Stay unassuming and open to new data.

Endeavor to learn at each opportunity; however, don't be know it all. You can't learn on the off chance that you starting at now think you know everything. Information is a middle Stoic restraint, and part of developing knowledge is conceding that you have far to go.

- Educate yourself at whatever point you can by understanding books, tuning in to web recordings, watching narratives, and perusing how-to guides.

- You could check out digital recordings like TEDTalks, RadioLab, and StarTalk Radio. Examine Netflix and various organizations for narratives on subjects like nature, advancement, and workmanship.

- If you have to scrutinize progressively about the Stoic perspective, the contemporary realist William B. Irvine is the main voice. His composing is open and doesn't use lots of difficult to reach philosophical language.

Concentrate on being sensible as opposed to being severe.

A veritable stoic isn't keen on enthusiastic clashes, requital, retribution, or holding sentiments of disdain. However, that doesn't mean you should be a chilly, evacuated, segregated sulk. In the event that somebody wrongs you, you can at present have compassion toward them whether or not you don't attract them in an enthusiastic clash.

- For model, in the event that somebody you care about lashes out at you, don't straightforwardly treat them with chilling hatred. You could state, "I don't believe it's shrewd just to hurl affronts forward and in reverse. We should put aside some push to chill off so we can deal with this circumstance judiciously."

- "Don't get upset, dole out the retribution," isn't at all stoic, so never endeavor to look for revenge. In case you're a boss answerable for reproving a specialist, think about a sensible strategy to think of them as dependable rather than aimlessly rebuffing them.

Attempting Stoic Meditations

Envision your place in the world.

The Hierocles' Circle is a Stoic visualization practice that causes you to consider how you fit into the great arrangement of things. Start by envisioning yourself, by then envision your family and colleagues around you. Picture your associates, neighbors, and partners in the accompanying circle, your city in the accompanying and, unavoidably, the entirety of mankind, the entirety of Nature, and the entirety of the nearness.

- Take around 10 minutes to do the action. On the off chance that it energizes you focus, sits in a serene spot, close your eyes, and take moderate, full breaths.

- The point is to value that things are interconnected. You're a bit of an informal organization and, eventually, connected to the entire universe.

Take a stab at envisioning an incredible setback.

A premeditation Malorum is a Stoic meditation wherein you envision losing something that is fundamental to you, similar to your action or a companion or relative. Picture a negative circumstance in your mind just for two or three minutes or something like that. It sounds upsetting, yet the fact is to recognize fleetingness, plan for blocks, consider the valuable things throughout your life, and defeat your sentiments of fear.

• Negative visualization can help produce mental quality, notwithstanding uncontrollable impediments. That suggests when something awful happens, you may have a simpler time adapting in the event that you've quite recently envisioned it.

Peruse a step by step quote and think about its importance.

Consistently, investigate a short quote by a Stoic researcher. We should accept it on various events to yourself and consider its importance. Whether or not it was made more than 2,000 years back, consider how you could apply its importance to your own one of a kind life.

- You could look online for articulations by scholars like Epictetus, Seneca, and Marcus Aurelius.

- You can likewise discover proclamations, reflections, and various resources on wise online diaries.

Compose an intelligent journal entry at the piece of the deal. At the piece of the deal, explain the challenges you stood up to and the choices you made. Examine a negative personal conduct standard you attempted to improve. Consider how you could have chosen a predominant choice or dealt with a circumstance in an unexpected way.

• For example, you may communicate, "Today Sam was short with me. I started to state something back yet got myself before I lost my cool. I'm showing signs of improvement about not permitting others to get under my skin, yet at the same time, have some work to do."

Applying Stoic Principles to Life

Try not to burn through your time on distractions.

Your time is important, so put forth an attempt not to sit around idly on mindless distractions. It might be intense in the present irate world, however, concentrate on what you're doing when you're playing out an undertaking or action. Whether or not you're only sitting without anyone else or conversing with a buddy, revolve around the moment as opposed to checking your telephone at ordinary interims.

• In expansion, put forth an attempt not to pester distractions like world news, ongoing improvements, and fiascoes. It's one thing to be educated about overall events. However, you don't want to weight or free for all about things you can't control.

Try not to perspire the little stuff.

Look at life's colossal challenges as opportunities to transform into a progressively canny, more grounded individual. With respect to the little unsettling influences, from spilled milk to losing five dollars, just endeavor to attempt to abstain from freezing.

• Your veritable sentiments of peacefulness are worth more than worrying over something of little worth. As the Stoic scholar Epictetus expressed, "A bit of spilled oil, a little taken wine - rehash to yourself, 'For such a little worth, I buy quietness.'"

Welcome the event.

You shouldn't be a stone-hued Scrooge to show circumspection and focus on right here and now. You can, regardless, acknowledge diversion, life's delights, and nature's greatness.

• For model, when given a glass of fine wine, a stoic individual may taste it and ponder, "Imagine a scenario where this is the last glass of wine I'll ever have?" The fact of the matter isn't that they're contemplating fate and anguish, yet that they value this special depiction of enjoyment.

Circle yourself with people you respect.

Being stoic doesn't mean you should separate yourself from others. Regardless, you should endeavor to contribute your significant vitality with people who should be progressively keen, choose better choices, and make you should be a prevalent individual.

• You don't want to be a self-important elitist, however, consider your associates and colleagues. Do they think of you as answerable for your actions, ask you to learn, and persuade you to develop yourself? Is there any individual who is negligible, critical, shrewd, or terrible?

Spot morals over material addition and acknowledgment.

The nature of your character is verifiably more critical than wealth, awards, or acclaim. Choose choices dependent on your moral principles as opposed to accomplishing something deceitful that improves your status.

- For model, don't help somebody since you need a prize or honor. Help them since it's the best possible activity, and don't gloat about it or search for consideration.

- Suppose lying about an associate would empower you to show up an advancement. A certified stoic wouldn't design something tricky just to get a raise.

HOW TO BE STRONGER AND THANKS TO THE STOICISM LESSON LEARNT

Here are some Stoic principles to take advantage of for an all the more fulfilling life:

Time is your most important resource

We know on a legitimate premise that our time is limited. Notwithstanding, the manner in which that the more noteworthy piece of us live is restricting that. We burn through quite a while at employments we abhor, stay with individuals we're not totally happy to be with, and, by and large, recognize conditions that don't cause us to feel pleased.

Remind yourself as a rule that time is your most significant resource. You have so long to live, so attempt determinedly to live to such an extent that will leave you with no apprehensions.

Apply what you understand

These days, it's anything but difficult to use huge measures of data and get learning. Regardless, there's besides no association between's get-together learning and genuine achievement.

You have to attempt to apply what you understand adequately. Not the only thing that is important, clearly, yet when you read a book or get the hang of something that improves your specialty, take cautious notes and make a game plan for applying that newfound data.

If you apply this principle, over and over, it will wind up being a bit of you. That is the point at which you advantage from the data.

Be thankful for what you have.

The advantages of thankfulness are by, and by bolstered by inquiring about, however, Marcus Aurelius and various Stoics examined its capacity ages before us. Continuously should be grateful whatever you have. The thing isn't to care for all you have or that you won't obtain more, but since of the adjustment in the mindset that appreciation makes. Appreciation swings the mind from "I need," "I need a greater amount of" and "I wish I had" to "I'm so sprightly I have," "I'm grateful I'm" and "I'm upbeat I could."

The effort basic to change this is immaterial. However, the distinction by the manner in which you feel after some time is awesome.

Be accessible

The capacity to inconspicuously be with yourself, tranquility present and mindful of what's going on around you, is a sign you have locked in on the idea of your mind.

In any case, the cool thing is, you can start practicing this now with no establishment or getting ready at all. Basically, stop for a moment to be with yourself tactfully. Monitor the feeling of breath on your lips, sensations in the body, the rising of your chest, and any substantial encounters around you, for instance, passing cars or splendid light.

To be at the time is a powerful encounter loaded with benefits. Exploit it

Make an effort not to look for satisfaction in the material.

Over the top authenticity is basically one more sign of what I call "the void"– it's an eventual outcome of the inclination that something is missing inside us, something we continue loading up with material things.

The thing is, the likelihood that material things satisfy us was made by advancement people endeavoring to sell more things. It's not founded on any legitimate information or logical research. Without a doubt, it feels incredible when we go from not having enough to having the choice to bear the cost of the expense of things we've never asserted, however, that is a compact kind of joy that can scarcely be seen as certifiable happiness.

The mind is your capacity.

Something that has helped Stoicism resurge in deference is that it shares much for all intents and purpose with the philosophy that frequently accompanies mindfulness meditation.

This principle has an inseparable tie to self-mindfulness, and understanding that by controlling your mind, you're prepared to live a progressively upbeat, progressively quiet life.
 You can work to impact outside conditions. However, that is an exertion that is clashing, the ideal situation. By figuring out how to ace the mind, you'll find your life and comprehend a power unquestionably more noticeable than anything outside yourself.

Recall your why

At the point when you're moving in the direction of a major objective, making sense of you're the reason that is, the explanation you need what you're advancing towards is one of the fundamental things of all.

Not as much since it motivates you when things are acceptable; however, it's more since realizing why you're buckling down aids you hold tight when things turn out badly.

Consider how you burn through your effort.

On some arbitrary day, what measure of time do you spend towards what is significant most to you? Burning through the effort with your family? Tackling your claim to fame? Managing yourself?

Do you experience hours by means of online life? Tattle locales? Haphazardly glancing through Reddit until you comprehend an hour has passed by, and you've done nothing beneficial?

High-achievers will when all is said in done, be staggering at arranging what is generally imperative to them, so consider what you burn through your effort doing and make the basic changes to comprehend the existence you had constantly needed.

See that all that we experience begins from inside.

It's not entirely obvious that all that we experience occurs in the space between our ears: outrage, distress, bliss, harmony, overthinking, stress, dread, re-thinking, lament, certainty, and everything in the middle.

Our emotions depict our encounters. What's more, it's in the cerebrum that we pick what emotions to react with established on those encounters.

See that all that we experience makes from inside, and you'll comprehend that you have altogether more control than your thought over how you feel on an ordinary premise.

Figure out how to manage the area of your emotions, and you'll make sense of how to ace a major piece of satisfaction.

Change your perspective on disillusionment.

It's entirely expected to believe the powerlessness to be negative. You've had a go at something, and it wasn't adequate. Regardless, your last crucial to be to transform into the perfect variation of yourself (and afterward utilizing that likelihood to serve others).

On the off chance that you investigate things as such, every failure transforms into a beneficial open entryway for self-improvement, a chance to use as a venturing stone to basically unavoidable accomplishment.

Have a good example to quantify your character

It's difficult to gauge your advancement as an individual without anything to quantify it against. Similarly, it's horrendous to gauge yourself against individuals who are not good idealistic examples.

You have to find someone that motivated you due to their colossal character, which connotes the characteristics you find generally required. When you've seen somebody you can try as like, you'll have a benchmark you can reliably use to measure your advancement.

5 Stoic Principles for Modern Living

Thought has been put into how life should be lived by the greeks, from Aristotle to Socrates to Plato, yet one of their most helpful perspectives stays misinterpreted by the greater part of the people: Stoicism. Notwithstanding Stoicism's undeserved reputation for being synonymous with coldness, it can incite an unbelievably satisfying lifestyle. Stoicism is an old perspective that can be cleaned by anyone to construct their rapture; various thoughts you may consider as now practice in your step by step participation.

Stoicism is, at its root, a perspective for restricting the negative emotions throughout your life and enhancing your thankfulness and joy; it fuses care practices and worth based living. Stoicism is a gadget to upgrade your human experience, both inside and remotely. Right now, share a part of the manners in which those Stoics think by explaining the noteworthiness behind a few their most notable pro's announcements. By uniting a piece of their perspectives into our regular day to day existences, I acknowledge we'll find more satisfaction in our step by step commitments and respond even more adaptably to issues and challenges that develop.

Standard 1: You can't change things outside of your control, yet you can change your attitude.

A key fragment of Stoicism is practicing care. See the events throughout your life that you do and don't have direction over. In the event that you become baffled with conditions outside of your control, you are wasting imperativeness and developing negative feelings. A Buddhist story best blueprints the stoic daily schedule with respect to protecting your mind from conditions out of your control. The enemy in the story is Mara, an adversary of the Buddha. Mara thought about the Buddha's powers and attempted to smash him, so he sent a mind-boggling, equipped power. Mara taught the troopers to hurl blazing rocks at the Buddha, yet when they drew near to him, they went to blooms and fell. Buddha's adversary by then prepared the military to shoot jolts at the Buddha, anyway again, the jolts pushed toward turning out to bloom once they gravitated toward to the Buddha's circle. There was nothing Mara could do to hurt the Buddha in light of the fact that the Buddha had aced the capacity to shield his bliss from outside events. I draw equal the stones and rushes to negative thoughts about outside conditions. You can't change these events; you can change your outlook towards them. Through this affirmation, our mind can end up safe. Since we can control our mindsets and reactions, we can very well never be oppositely affected by outside events.

Rule 2: Don't fall prey to current society's materialistic nature.

Our consumerist society seems to make more need than it fulfills. These results in everyone are remaining mindful of the Jones' — yet it's questionable that even the Jones' are chipper. Our steady prologue to media and advancing keeps us requiring and seeing better out there — we spend our merited money on the latest winning design, convinced it will leave us fulfilled until structure 2.0 diverts out one year from now. On the off chance that we attempt to unnecessary, our aching reduces, and we become progressively content with what we have, which conveys us to the accompanying articulation.

Standard 3: Picture existence without the people and resources you have to esteem them.

We've seen now that requiring more prompts dissatisfaction — so how might we find satisfaction? The key lies in appreciation. We should respect all that we have and find a rapture in it. We live in a mind-boggling time of history with basic access to necessities and advancement that gives a lifestyle that was unforeseeable just two or three pages back. Instead of esteeming this, we think little of One stoic practice is to imagine that you lost a segment of your noteworthy assets. It may sound debilitating from the start; be that as it may, by imagining these setbacks, we come to recognize what we have more. It's fundamental that we not put an abundance of need on the things we have either — for they may not generally be there. Being Stoic strategies finding joy through whatever you do have — in case you place emphasis on an outside thing and it is evacuated, the stoic should not be upset yet rather grateful they had the thing regardless. Everything is acquired from the universe. Mass ventures all over. Be that as it may, goodness remains, and in that misrepresentations bliss.

Rule 4: Be truly coordinated in the sum of your joint efforts.

We at present understand that euphoria starts from inside and from recognizing everything around us — despite something as clear as living at a point in time where we can buy separated water for $1.00 from a treat machine near 100 feet from us (We genuinely think little of things sometimes). Since, with the stoic viewpoint, our bliss can end up liberated from various factors, we ought to be happy all the time as stoics since we don't need anything over human experience. If we needed more, we could empower ourselves to be disappointed. This doesn't suggest that Stoics can't value the better things throughout everyday life — it just methods we shouldn't think of them as fundamental for our satisfaction. Simply offering goodness to the world through helping people and pushing society — something we each can do once per day — can make us fulfilled.

Rule 5: Practicing your characteristics beats addressing them.

Stoic perspective requires an incredible course of action of good commitment. It isn't such a lot that you should be frantically hard on yourself, yet you should understand that every decision that you make for the day contains a moral estimation. Stoicism must be bored in the event that you have to affect the world in an unrivaled manner. Ask yourself, for the most part, "What's the perfect method to act right now?" should like to choose choices reliant on your characteristics to grow the more marvelous incredible. Live by your moral code.

I've eventually found that the exercises of Stoicism, at whatever point practiced, can fabricate our satisfaction. Stoicism isn't a "win huge or forget about it;" don't stop for a second to pick t parts of Stoicism would best impact your life.

WHY STOICISM IS PERFECT AND MODERN FOR MANAGERS

Stoicism, despite everything, has a gigantic add up to show us, particularly in these enthusiasm immersed times. Furthermore, the Stoic heritage has molded our reality in a bigger number of ways than you may anticipate. Here are five reasons why Stoicism matters:

Bill Clinton has gotten for his epic. Apparently, half-advertisement libbed show stem-winder, one of the most noteworthy lines has hardly earned a notice using any and all means. We were astounded to hear Clinton called Barack Obama "a man cool outwardly, yet who expends for America within."

Alright, dismiss the "consuming for America part," which is soft even by Bubba benchmarks. What's intriguing here is that President Obama truly expected somebody to go in front of an audience and vouch for his energy—to demand that, in fact, it was in there somewhere. Most open figures are, generally, outward energy, all backslapping, love presses, and barely controlled tears.

"Cool outwardly" is something Americans rarely find in an administration official; less unselfish onlookers look at the equal presidential quality and see "detachedness," "standoffishness," "grandiosity," and even the incomparable American sin of not being "a people person."

Once in a while, apparently, we don't understand how to process an administration official who wears emotions wherever other than on his sleeve.

Be that as it may, Clinton's line on Obama struck an unmistakable congruity for us since we've spent the recent years considering and composing on another administration official famous for his coolness: Cato the Younger.

He was a professional of Stoicism, and out of date Greek religion that he brought to Rome. We aren't guaranteeing that the president's a secret Stoic. Be that as it may, we do believe that the open reaction to his limitation shows how insufficiently Stoic attributes can go over in our events: a perspective dependent on enthusiastic control seems, by all accounts, to be unusual in the hour of over-sharing.

We feel that it is disfavor. Stoicism, despite everything, has an enormous signify, show us, especially in these enthusiasm soaked events. In addition, the Stoic legacy has shaped our existence in a more noteworthy number of ways than you may foresee. Here are five reasons why Stoicism matters:

Stoicism is made for globalization.

The world that delivered Stoicism was a parochial, frequently xenophobic detect. In the event that is clearly grasping those divisions sounds unconventional to us, we have Stoicism to thank. It was maybe the essential Western perspective to address comprehensive partnership. Epictetus said that all of us are our own one of a kind local land, yet "additionally a person from the extraordinary city of celestial creatures and men."

In the event that the best approach to bliss is really in our own special wills, by then, even the best social allotments start to look inconsequential. The Roman Stoic Seneca lived in an overall population dependent on subjection, yet he additionally urged his related Romans to "review that he whom you call your slave sprang from a comparative stock, is smiled upon by comparative skies, and on proportionate terms with yourself inhales, lives, and passes on."

This grip of cosmopolitanism made Stoicism the ideal perspective for the Roman Empire, which brought an excellent extent of races and religions into contact. Stoicism appeared to be great for a globalized world- - in any case, it does.

It's a perspective for power.

Stoicism teaches us that, before we endeavor to control events, we have to control ourselves first. Our endeavors to apply the effect on the world are at risk of probability, frustration, and dissatisfaction - yet control of oneself is the main kind that can succeed 100% of the time. From head Marcus Aurelius on, pioneers have found that a Stoic frame of mind picks up them respect even with frustration, and watchmen against affectedness despite accomplishment.

Clearly, Stoicism doesn't guarantee results. One of Bill Clinton's favored books was Marcus Aurelius' Meditations- - and he's no one's concept of a Stoic. Cato, the Younger, became tied up with thusly of deduction from his young adulthood to his demise. However, he was likewise inclined to vicious changes of irateness, obstinate pride, and intermittent intoxication.

Stoicism has an interest in any individual who faces vulnerability - that is, for every one of us. However, pioneers are especially liable to risk and progress, so it's not astounding that countless them locate a Stoic mentality significant to their enthusiastic prosperity. We referenced Barack Obama's Stoic way above- - and there's some progressive verification for it in his continuous meeting with Michael Lewis. "I'm attempting to pare down choices," he told Lewis. "I don't want to choose choices about what I'm eating or wearing. Since I have too various choices to make...You need to routinize yourself. You can't be experiencing the day redirected by random data." Whatever your assessment of Obama's legislative issues, that is great Stoicism- - attempting to draw lines between the fundamental and the inessential at every level of life.

Anyway, in his most valiant minutes - when he looked down the military of Julius Caesar and unavoidable destruction without flickering - Cato experienced the Stoic great. The Stoics empowered that we bomb obviously more frequently than we succeed, that to be human is to be shocking, intolerant, and angry undeniably more regularly than we'd like. In any case, they likewise demonstrated a handy strategy to be more.

In case you're Christian, you're currently part-Stoic.

Envision a religion that concentrated on human organization under a philanthropic maker God; that instructed us to direct and ace our fundamental wants instead of surrendering to them; that by the by demanded that all individuals, since we're human, will without a doubt crash and burn at this strategic; that contributed a lot of vitality discussing "still, small voice" and the various perspectives, or "people," of a unitary God. Most of that may sound notable. However, the perspective that developed those thoughts was not Christianity yet Stoicism.

As Christianity kept on creating, church pioneers, who expected to accentuate the uniqueness of their certainty, began to make light of this Stoic association. In any case, Stoicism is still there at the establishment of the Christian religion, in a bit of its most fundamental terms and concepts.

It looks good that Christianity is a significantly Stoic religion. Stoicism commanded Roman culture for a long time—and Christianity went standard in comparative culture. What's dynamic, an extensive part of the pioneers of the early Christian church were previous Stoics. Clearly, Christianity procured a considerable amount of its thought and wording from Stoicism- - on the grounds that pondering religion in the mid-initial thousand years inferred taking on a similar mindset as a Stoic.

It was worked for extreme events.

Stoicism was imagined in a world falling isolated. Developed in Athens just several decades after Alexander the Great's triumphs and sudden passing overturned the Greek world, Stoicism took off on the grounds that it offered security and concordance in a time of battling and crisis. The Stoic articulation of confidence didn't ensure material security or concordance in life following death, yet it guaranteed relentless satisfaction right now.

The world may take everything from us; Stoicism uncovers to us that we all in all have a post within. The Stoic realist Epictetus, who was brought into the world a slave and debilitated at a youthful age, communicated: "Where is the incredible? In the will...If anybody is hopeless, allowed him to remember that he is pained by reason of himself alone."

Stoicism uncovers to us that no joy can be secure if it's built up inalterable, destructible things. Our money related can create or shrivel; our callings can succeed or wallow; even our loved ones can be taken from us. There is just one detect the world can't contact: our internal identities, our choice at every moment to be brave, to be sensible, to be incredible.

While it's normal to yell out at torment, the Stoic endeavors to stay unconcerned with everything that happens outwardly, to remain likewise chipper amidst triumph and catastrophe, it's a requesting way of life, yet the prize it offers is opportunity from energy - opportunity from the emotions that so regularly seem to control us when we should control them. A veritable Stoic isn't hardhearted. However, the individual has an authority of emotions, since Stoicism sees that fear or unreachability or despairing possibly enter our minds when we enthusiastically let them in.

Instructing like that seems, by all accounts, to be expected for a world tense, whether or not it's the wild universe of out of date Greece or a bleeding-edge money related crisis. Be that as it may, by then, Epictetus would express that- - as long as we endeavor to place our joy is short-lived things- - our universes are reliably restless.

It's the individual philosophy of the military.

In 1965, James Stockdale's A-4E Skyhawk was shot down over Vietnam. He later remembered the moment like this: "After discharge, I had around thirty seconds to possess my last articulation in an open door before I landed...And so help me, I murmured to myself: 'Five years down there, in any event. I'm leaving the universe of advancement and entering the universe of Epictetus.'"

Stockdale was not the only one as a military man who drew quality from Stoicism. In her book The Stoic Warrior, Nancy Sherman, who indicated reasoning at the Naval Academy, battled that Stoicism is a main impetus behind the military mindset- - especially in its accentuation on duration, limitation, and inward quality. As Sherman makes, at whatever point her perspective class at Annapolis went to the Stoic scholars, "various officials and understudies the same felt they had gotten back home."

Stockdale experienced more than seven years in a Vietnamese jail, and he made that Stoicism saved his life. Stockdale had experienced years concentrating Stoic thought before conveying, and he pulled in those lessons to manage his detainment. These words from Epictetus kept returning to him: "Do you not understand that life is a warrior's service?... If you dismiss your obligations when some genuine solicitation is laid upon you, do you not comprehend what a forsaken state you bring the military?" While a segment of his related POWs tormented themselves with fake any wants for an early discharge, Stockdale's Stoic practice helped him stand up to the horrendous truth of his circumstance, without surrendering to despair and discouragement.

The more we practice Stoic qualities on incredible events, the more likely that we'll see them in ourselves when they're commonly required.

GENERAL REASON TO PRACTICE STOIC AND UNIVERSAL GUIDE

General Reason – The Guide to Stoic Practice

What portrayed a Stoic paying little mind to whatever else was the choice of real existence wherein every thought, each craving, and every action would be guided by no other law than that of general Reason?

The Stoics set a sensible, divine, and lucky universe at the point of convergence of their philosophical structure and relied upon it as a guide for all their thoughts, need, and movement. For the Stoic, Nature is the extent of all things. As an outpouring of comprehensive Reason (logos), Nature gives the gauges we should live according to continue with a splendid (exemplary) life and experience a better than average stream or flourishing throughout everyday life (eudaimonia). As needs are, Stoicism doesn't empower us to get what we need throughout everyday life. Rather, it gives a proficient, philosophical lifestyle that urges how to get what we need—morals—so we can experience a satisfaction. As I raised in advance, Stoicism has compelled the capacity to impact change when we considerably add it to an actual existence stacked up with passionate pressure and driven by needs and hatreds. The stoic practice is anything but a topical ointment. Rather, it works from the back to the front. The stoic practice is a wrinkle that tunnels significant and turns the soil of upset minds upside down to reveal our befuddled insights and deluded needs and repugnances. Regardless, flipping around our lives is no essential task; it requires a complete change in context. We should come to see a real existence composed essentially without any other person's information centered considerations, needs, and exercises for what it is from the perspective of Stoicism—unnatural. Hadot prescribes this requires "a complete reversal of our standard method for looking" and fights,

This difference in vision begins when we step past speculation and start to practice what Hadot calls the "significant exercises" of old philosophy. It was seen that bleeding edge inclinations might make some object to the articulation "powerful" in principle. Regardless, as he points out, no other term covers the extensiveness of these outdated practices, which loosen up past irrelevant plans to incorporate "the individual's entire psychism."

These exercises, including the astuteness or Reason, be that as it may, most of an individual's assets, including feeling and imaginative mind, had a comparable target as all old perspective: diminishing human torment and extending satisfaction, by training people to withdraw themselves from their particular, egocentric, individualistic viewpoints and become mindful of their having a spot, as irreplaceable fragment parts, to the Whole settled by the entire universe.

Stoic practice not simply incorporates the 'entire psychism' of the person. Be that as it may, it also requires the relationship of every one of the three bits of the sweeping Stoic structure—justification, material science, and ethics—which concur with comprehensive Reason.

For the Stoics, a comparative Reason was crushing endlessly in NatureNature (and material science), in the informal community (and ethics), and unique thought (and method of reasoning). The single exhibit of the intellectual in getting ready for savvy right now to blend with the exceptional showing of far-reaching Reason, which is accessible inside all things and in accordance with itself.

For the Stoic, these exercises join the attitude of thought (prosocial), and the three Stoic requests (assent, need, and action). I clarified this as of now in the course of action titled The Path of the Prokopton. Through the demonstration of these significant exercises, "the individual raises himself to the life of the objective Spirit; at the end of the day, he replaces himself with the perspective of the Whole." This self-important point of view consistently implied as a view from above gives the expert another disposition toward the events throughout their life.

The rationalist must give up his deficient, glad vision of this present reality, all together, by method for material science, to rise to the point of believing things to be across the board Reason sees them. Above all, the pragmatist ought to healthily wish the advantage of all of the universe and society. By finding that an area can have no other authentic extraordinary than the advantage of the entirety of the All.

Seen inside the setting of for as far back as they can recollect, and the Whole of the universe, events once thought to be hazardous, or even deplorable, take on new significance. From this point of vi, we begin to understand the Stoic standard that it isn't events that issue us, yet our insights about those events (Enchiridion 16). This distinction in setting or change of vision is developed through the preparation known as the control of need. As Hadot notes:

The power of want involves in re-putting oneself inside the setting of the tremendous All, and in finding a good pace of human nearness like a segment. One that must fit in with the craving of the Whole, which for this circumstance is proportionate to general Reason.

Thereafter, while explaining the request for need, it highlighted the manner in which that this controls us to consent to "Fate":

As we have seen, the exercises of the significance of oneself and spotlight on the present, together with our consent to the craving of Nature as it appears in each event, raise our insight to a huge level. By consenting to the here and now which is coming to pass, in which the whole world is surmised, I need what broad Reason needs and perceive myself with it in my conclusion of collaboration and of having a spot with a Whole which transcends the cutoff purposes of singularity.

Hadot depicts the effect of this pompous point of view as seeks after:

Our perspective is changed eventually when oneself, as a standard of chance, sees that there is nothing more huge than the moral extraordinary, and right now what has been willed by Destiny, at the end of the day, far-reaching Reason.

In the opening proclamation of this post, Pierre Hadot certifies that "across the board Reason" controls all of the Stoic practices. To proceed, we need to grasp what Hadot suggests by general Reason and how it can fill in as a guide for Stoic practice. Portrays of comprehensive Reason are:

- That which gives "structure and imperativeness to give that is surrendered."

- The wellspring of "reason which is essential to all humankind and ensures its."

- The "will" of Nature we are to seek after

- A tendency toward "self-discernment."

- "God is nothing other than general Reason."

- eUniversal Reason is the whole of which our discerning clarification is an area.

- The "will" that "basically" associates all events

- The "phenomenal Norm which sets the complete estimation of significant quality."

- "the logos [reason] which connects all through all things."

- Something the Epicureans kept the nearness from verifying.

- The "direct" or "circumlocutory" Reason for all "things and events."

- That which "wills" our Destiny.

- The extraordinary guide for a Stoic life

General Reason is the "law" trademark in target reality, which can be known in light of the fact that our human characters are the aftereffect of that identical comprehensive Reason. The Stoics asserted there is target truth (law) and an objective standard of significant quality, and we are reliant upon that law and moral standard.

The Stoic sage realizes a comparative satisfaction as general Reason, which is allegorically epitomized by Zeus; for divine creatures and people share an equivalent clarification, which is faultless in the awesome creatures yet perfectible in individuals. The sage has accomplished the faultlessness of depiction by making his inspiration coordinate with divine Reason and mixing his will with the eminent will.

While simply Stoic sage can have perfect learning of fantastic Reason that creation progress on the Stoic way (the prokopton) can at present use our poor appreciation of comprehensive Reason as a manual forever. Presenting such a defense quickly opens the door to fundamentalists in both religion and science who ensure they have specific access to such truth. Incidentally, that is a significant risk considering the elective, which swarms the forefront West—the all-out repudiation of target truth. The Stoics recognized that objective reality, and, right now, truth exists. In like way, they battle that our happiness must be found in an undertaking, in any case defective, to understand and live according to that boundless Reason. This is the excursion of the never-ending perspective, found in all sagacity shows.

The Stoics recognized that general Reason (logos) is the Reason for the universe, and our human characters are molded by that proportional Reason in such a manner, that empowers us to grasp the world in which we live. These unprovable suppositions (maxims) underlie current science too. Science for all intents and purposes acknowledges, yet can't effectively illustrate that reality exists. Figuratively speaking, this isn't a dream or a trick by a Cartesian underhandedness soul. In like way, science expects the fact of the matter is sensible, and we are prepared for understanding it to some degree. Without these assumptions, we are everlastingly stuck in solipsism or lost in a vacuous relativism. With trust in those focal adages, mankind has researched and insightfully thought about the universe. We have amassed volumes of learning, and we have improved human life in a load of ways. Regardless, the demonstration of science, by its very nature, is compelled to the 'how' requests concerning reality. It is unequipped for taking note of the enormous 'why' questions like: is there any significance or Reason to most of this? Is our discernment, which can address and explore itself, the eventual outcome of understanding or blessed shot? Is it ordinary to state that we are permitted to pick our reactions to our condition and right now, mindful?

The Stoics fought with those proportionate requests in outdated events. One instance of their fight to answer 'why' questions appear in the conversation over the possibility of the universe. The 'fortune or particles' disjunction in Stoicism includes the investigating and existential choice between two undeniable world-sees. Marcus' proceeded with treatment of that disjunction in his Meditations shows three apparent certainties. In the first place, a fortune made a distinction to Marcus and the Stoics. If it didn't have any kind of effect, Marcus and Seneca would not have repeated it as they did. Second, Marcus' proceeded with treatment of this disjunction shows lowliness toward what is reasonable with any degree of conviction. In two or three sections, Marcus even appears to communicate powerlessness about which of the world-sees is fairly legitimate. Neither one of the world's see—fortune or particles—can be 'illustrated' through the specific system. The printed verification suggests that the Stoics straightforwardly thought about how possible it is that they couldn't be correct, and the Epicurean world-view could be right. Finally, in disdain their defenselessness, the Stoics chose the existential choice to put resources into a luckily mentioned universe as a proverb and a short time later develop their philosophical system around that doubt.

He battles that Marcus' reiterated verification of the 'arrangement or atoms' subject was "regular inside the Stoic school" and not his creation. The Stoics, Hadot fights, used this conflict to "develop evidently that, whether or not Epicureanism was substantial—a hypothesis which they dismissed totally—one would at present need to live like a Stoic." Regardless of whether the Epicureans are correct, and the universe is the result of lucky probability, one ought to at present "go about according to reason, and accept moral extraordinary to be the primary incredible." As Hadot raises here and elsewhere, "Such a position doesn't propose doubt—an unbelievable inverse."

By imagining that their physical hypotheses might be bogus and that people would, regardless, need to live as Stoics. They revealed what, in their eyes, was critical to their structure. What described a Stoic paying little heed to whatever else was the choice of real existence wherein every thought, each hankering, and every movement would be guided by no other law than that of general Reason. Whether or not the world is mentioned or tempestuous, it relies just upon us to be wisely discerning with ourselves.

Hadot then gives the most minimal and capable assessment of the 'fortune or particles' theme I have found. He communicates that "all of the teachings of Stoicism gets from this existential choice." He is implying the choice between the sensible, luckily, mentioned the universe of the Stoics and the discretionary universe of the Epicureans. The Stoic path relies upon the existential decision to consider them to be as sensible and deliberate. In what capacity can the Stoics support such a supposition? According to Hadot, the Stoics expressed,

It is unimaginable that the universe could make human sensibility, with the exception of if the last were by then in some way or another or another present inside the previous.

Amusingly, when we fast forward twenty-300 years, we wind up looking with the proportional existential choice. Additionally, a comparative hole exists today among momentum masterminds and analysts as they attempt to explain, or explain away, human mindfulness and the express solicitation of the universe. Reductionists fight that cognizance is just what the cerebrum does. Thusly, it is an epiphenomenon, a reaction, or a mental trip made by neural strategies. Fortunately, a normally extending number of researchers are trying this pragmatist model by setting that perception must be a focal piece of reality itself. A bit of these researcher is making disputes which sound astoundingly like Stoic speculation.

Anyway, what do most of this mean for a twenty-first-century master of Stoicism? It suggests you have a fundamental comparative choice today as the individuals of yesteryear did—either fortune or atoms. Either there is a piece of subtle information inside the universe, or the world is the result of the shot. Neither one of the choices is provable, nor does setting our trust in either requires a demonstration of unadulterated confidence. Regardless, the choice isn't among science and religion; that is a fake division presented by fundamentalists on the different sides to impact people in the middle to their remarkable position. Various sharp people, over a wide period, agree to the nearness of information inside the surface of the universe without getting tied up with any appropriate strict conviction or practice. There is a large space between traditional religion and suspicion held by various savvy masterminds over a wide period. Einstein made it extremely clear he was neither a nonbeliever nor a follower to any traditional religion. Like the Stoics, Einstein didn't believe in an individual God; regardless, he certified that individuals could climb to a "third period of strict experience" he called "interminable religion" where,

The individual feels the uselessness of human needs and focuses and the sublimity and great solicitation which reveal themselves to both in thee Nature and to the domain of thought. Particular nearness interests him as a sort of prison, and he needs to experience the universe as a solitary vital entirety.

Everybody who is really drawn in with the journey for science twists up convinced that some spirit appears in the laws of the universe, one that is enormously superior to that of man. Thusly, the journey for science prompts a strict assessment of a one of a kind sort, which is irrefutably very not exactly equivalent to the strictness of someone progressively credulous.

Einstein extensively formed that he put confidence in "Spinoza's God, who reveals himself in the exact agreeableness of what exists." Ironically, Spinoza's God is the polytheism of Stoicism. Another awe-inspiring mastermind, William James, when portrayed "religion in its broadest sense."

The conviction that there is a covered solicitation, and that our prevalent extraordinary lies in agreeably changing ourselves to that. This conviction and this adjustment are the strict attitudes in the spirit.

Again, that could have been made by any out of the old Stoics. By and by, we can return to the huge existential choice of the Stoic, as conveyed by Pierre Hadot.

What described a Stoic to the avoidance of everything else was the choice of an actual existence where every thought, each hankering. What's more, every movement would be guided by no other law than that of a comprehensive Reason.

We individuals couldn't care less for unclearness and helplessness; likewise, we will as a rule slant toward limits which give bogus sureness. We see this in the propelled science versus religion chitchat, which is controlled by fundamentalists from the different sides. Sadly, reasonable people who try to grip a sound, yet significant, position in the no man's land between those delved in limits will, by and large, take fire from the different sides. Neither nonbelievers nor ordinary strict followers find the Stoic beginning of eminent Nature similarly as they would like.

The dedication of the Stoics didn't rely upon superstition or legend. The theory and practices of Stoicism are worked around the existential obligation to a luckily mentioned universe. Numerous moderns get hung up on the likelihood that they have to 'have trust' in the arrangement. It isn't about conviction; it is a choice—an existential duty. Everyone makes that obligation purposely or instinctively. The people who power at 'confidence' in the arrangement as often as possible disregard the way that they, as usual, 'acknowledge' the universe, and human comprehension is the result of a movement of infinitely unreasonable accidents. Like it or not, a demonstration of unadulterated trust is fundamental regardless. That existential duty was basic to the Stoics; it gave Marcus the psychological assurance and help to state,

Everything suits me that suits your structures, O my universe. Nothing is too early, or past the final turning point for me, that is in your own fantastic time.

Seneca pointed out the differentiation these world-sees make in a valuable, yet puncturing way,

Despite which is substantial, Lucilius, or regardless of whether they all are, we should see present work on reasoning. Possibly the unbendable law of Destiny obliges us; maybe God, the across the board official, manages all events; it is maybe chance that drives human endeavors, and upsets them: the same, it is reasoning that must ensure us.

Reasoning gives the fundamental wellspring of help for the existential request. Regardless, the choice between those world-sees has any impact on one's situation toward this present reality, and their consequent cerebrum examine. Seneca raises the qualification in unambiguous terms,

The reasoning will request that we give willing loyalty to God, but then a reluctant accommodation to fortune. It will train you to seek after God; to adjust to change.

Willing accommodation to a luckily mentioned universe or reluctant passive consent to the potential states of fortune. We should, like the attached canine in the eminent Stoic relationship, seek after the truck of Destiny. We choose to do so energetically or reluctantly. We, all in all, choose that choice—intentionally or unconsciously. A considerable number of individuals get pulled through life kicking and yelling; some become exhausted on being pulled and look for a choice. Stoicism gives another option.

The Stoics thought about the verification and translated that comprehensive Reason—divine prudence—is normally known to mankind. Reasonably, they wrapped up the insightful individual must convey their life into accord with that comprehensive Reason.

EXERCISE FOR MANAGERS TO BOOST POWER AND SELF-CONTROL

Stoic Exercises To Get You Started

Stoics practiced certain exercises and drew upon them for quality.

We should look at three of the most noteworthy such works out.

All Situations Have Their Inconveniences Bad Situations Don't Exist.

The Stoics had a movement called turning the Obstacle Upside Down. In the event that you haven't read it starting at now, read Ryan Holiday's book "The Obstacle Is The Way," which is in my Essential Stoic Reading List.

Here is the charm: If you can make enough flip around an issue, each "horrible" transforms into another wellspring of good.

Started a business, and it failed?

Taking everything into account, you've met with such coaches and adjusted such a noteworthy number of capacities along the way that there is nothing that gets you far from attempting again and improves this time.

Assume for a second that you are attempting to help somebody, and they react by being surly or reluctant to participate. Maybe you are attempting to make an association with a guide or business assistant.

Rather than making your life progressively troublesome, the action says, they're truly guiding yourself towards new morals; for example, persistence or comprehension.

The passing of somebody close to you is a chance to show courage. Incredible Roman sovereign, Marcus Aurelius portrayed it like this:

"The snag to action propels action. What holds up traffic transforms into the way."

The regular abstain about business visionaries is that they abuse, even make, openings. To the Stoic, everything is a chance.

A disappointing speak with your clients where your help goes undervalued, the passing of a companion or relative, none of those are "openings" in the common sentiment of the word. In all honesty, they are the inverse. They are obstructions.

What a Stoic does is change every obstacle into a possibility.

There is nothing worth referencing or dreadful to the rehearsing Stoic. There is just an observation.

You control discernments, not genuine events. Your understanding of events is completely in your control.

Mull over Your Death – It Awaits Us All

Marcus Aurelius stayed in contact with himself a clear and powerful reminder to help him recapture point of view and stay adjusted:

"Synopsis the once-over of the people who felt extreme disturbance at something: the most notable, the most disastrous, the most loathed, the most whatever: Where is such now? Smoke, buildup, legend… or not using any and all means a legend. Think about the significant number of models. Moreover, how unimportant the things we need so energetically are."

The Stoics talk about killing 'interests,' which they called apatheia; they suggest silly, bothersome, and irrational needs and emotions.

Remember the time you required something fanatically?

How huge would those needs look if you somehow happened to kick the can tomorrow? By and by, you may state:

"Be that as it may, Arda, I can't carry on with my life as though I'll kick the container tomorrow! If I somehow happened to do that, I'd state screw you to everything and just play PC games for the duration of the day." Here is the thing.

Considering our passing makes us carry clearness to what is huge in the event that you feel you'd basically drop everything and play PC games, perhaps in spite of all that you haven't found your life's inspiration.

Here is the thing that is doing what you value feels like:

"Whether or not I was to fail horrendously tomorrow, I'd, regardless, do that action, make that video, make that book, paint that moment, play that piano piece. Seeking after my life's inspiration and inventive commitment is that wonderful for me."

To extraordinary emotions, the shock would be a veritable model.

You may believe that it is normal to feel shocked. It is in our human intuition, right?

Surely and no. Since the shock is a characteristic of human feeling, it doesn't suggest that you should enjoy it.

What high does it stop by getting angry?

It doesn't care for the sentiment of disarray when you may discover a sort of elective arrangement, nor is it like gratefulness where you pat yourself on the back and remind yourself how lucky you are.

Shock makes us sincerely hopeless, just as it harms the people around us.

How regularly have you wished you didn't express that word? You could've stated it much better. Be that as it may, while furious, you can't think straight and regret your actions subsequently.

The outcomes of hatred are outrageous to such a degree that it doesn't justify the satisfaction you may get by letting yourself explode.

Seek after a progressively capable alternative. Make sense of how to calm yourself. Keep an even stoop. Be pragmatic.

Coming back to the point of the movement, it's basic: recall how little you are.

Why explode or debilitate when the universe couldn't mindless in any way, shape, or form?

You and your issues are just little residue particles in the world, before long be wrecked by death.

By and by, you may ask: If everything is vaporous, what does have any kind of effect?

Right now matters. Being a conventional individual and doing the best thing right now, that is the thing that issues, and that is what was fundamental to the Stoics.

Take Alexander the Great, who vanquished the known world and had urban networks named in his respect. This is general data. Here is something you most likely won't have heard.

Once while alcoholic, Alexander got into a fight with his dearest partner, Cleitus, and unexpectedly killed him.

A short time later, he was despairing to such a degree that he was unable to eat or drink for three days. Pundits were brought from all over Greece to see what they could do about his torment, to no profit.

Is this the trait of a successful life? Is this really what you need?

It makes a difference little when you get all the cash and assets on the planet If you lose the point of view and hurt everybody around you.

Addition from Alexander's mistake. Be unobtrusive and fair, and mindful. That is something you can have every single day of your life. You'll never need to fear somebody taking it from you or, all the more dreadful still, it assumes control over you.

Negative Visualization + Application

Seneca, who had a great time extraordinary wealth as the expert of Nero, prescribed that we should set aside a specific number of days consistently to practice neediness. Take a little sustenance, wear your most perceptibly horrible pieces of clothing, make tracks the other way from the solace of your home and bed. Put yourself very close with need, and he expressed, you'll ask yourself, "Is this what I used to fear?"

People are altered to look for after two conditions of minds: solace and security.

Look at your ordinary actions, what number of them are done trying to make solace or security?

I bet all of them essentially.

Solace is the most discernibly awful sort of bondage since you're constantly anxious that a person or thing will evacuate it. Security makes us sincere and delicate. It is more brilliant to put ourselves in not actually ideal circumstances as a way to deal with toughening ourselves.

In the event that you were bound to a poor family, amazing! You can give yourself certainty and the importance of steady work as it so happens throughout everyday life.

In the event that your movement makes you have to butcher yourself, amazing! By and by, you can plunk down, think about, and discover your life's inspiration.

On the off chance that your darling/playmate makes you crazy, fantastic! Conceivably the opportunity has arrived to consider your relationship genuinely. Will you impart and deal with your issues or discover an undeniably fitting assistant?

Montaigne was enamored with an old drinking game where the people alternated holding up a work of art of a body inside a casket and cheered "Drink and are glad for when you're dead you will take after this."

Emotions like pressure and fear have their hidden establishments in vulnerability and once in while inability.

As Seneca says, "We persevere through more in our creative mind than this present reality."

Any individual who has made a significant bet on themselves knows how much essential anxiety and fear can expend.

The arrangement is to deal with that negligence. Make yourself familiar with the things, the most cynical situation circumstances, that you're restless about.

Practice what you fear, whether or not a reproduction in your mind or, taking everything into account.

Remember: the drawback is regularly reversible or short-enduring.

Some Stoic Exercises for Impressive Self-Improvement

- **Consider Yourself Dead**

This is from Marcus Aurelius: "Consider yourself dead. You have carried on with your life. By and by taking what's left and live it appropriately."

This can be deciphered in an unexpected way. It migtht be a negative visualization about the most horrible that could happen, which is demise. It could plan to overlook all that happened previously and live just in right here and now. Try not to worry over the past and make the best of today. Today is all you have. Value it and make its best.

I believe it's an incredible instrument to not settling on any unpredictable choices and actions. It urges you to base on the extremely huge with the objective that you don't sit around on trifles yet just on fundamentals.

Use your time. Likewise, this isn't in the Yolo sense. . You have an occupation. Your obligation is to be an extraordinary individual, to endeavor your best, and to carry on with the existence of reason and goals.

If it doesn't have any kind of effect on what crap you have done previously. Life is new now. You can't fix what you have done, however in any case, and you have the chance to be the perfect individual.

Action: You spent on the previous evening and are at present given a subsequent shot on earth. Make two records:

1. What are the most noteworthy things throughout your life?
2. What do you truly contribute your vitality with? Consider the summaries and pick one thing you will upgrade in the next days.

- **Remind Yourself of the Impermanence of Things**

We don't generally have things. Your vehicle can be taken. Your home can catch fire. You can lose your hair, to be sure, even your body.

Try not to get appended to things; they do eventually not have any kind of effect. Your favored shirt? A touch of wool… The Stoics go well beyond. They state, don't get excessively appended to your loved ones. Epictetus expressed, "When giving your adolescent or spouse a kiss, rehash to yourself, 'I am kissing a human.'"

Life is transient, and people we care about may be grabbed from all of us of an unexpected and abruptly. Additionally, you yourself are mortal. You could pass on tomorrow.

Remind yourself how significant life is right now, and how important your loved ones are, on the grounds that they may before long be gone. Acknowledge what you have and remind yourself of the temporariness of things.

Action: Take one moment to think about your own mortality. Life on earth is confined, it is possibly procured, and you don't have a clue when you have to return it. Use it and reliably review, "You are mortal, your loved ones are mortal."

- **Mirror your day**

This is fundamental yet effective.

You may call it journaling. The thought is to reflect yourself. What extraordinary did you do today?

What might you have the option to improve?

What's more, by what means may you be basically the best form?

That is a form I read about recently. The extraordinary, better, best reflection. This is extraordinary on the grounds that you need to go over the things you recently did incredibly. This is rousing and fortifying you're extraordinary muscles.

The best is probably going to record things. Be that as it may, it is definitely not a need. By and by, I record my destinations and execution goals for the next day. That is a little affinity that is anything but difficult to remain mindful of. Hence I don't record my impressions of the day at the present time.

I go quickly during my time reliably, just in my mind. Moreover, its things are gigantic. I am progressively mindful for the duration of the day, and I separate very soon when I don't act like I believe was perfect. This is fundamentally a mindfulness instrument.

Action: Commit to the incredible, better, best reflection for one week's worth of work. Take 5 minutes consistently before you hit the roughage and ask yourself these 3 direct inquiries. This action alone can do you enormous help, similar to individual progression.

- **Intentional Discomfort – Lay on the Floor in Starbucks**

Resolute inconvenience: Train for awkward circumstances so you won't jump when they come.

This is tied in with getting awkward to build up your customary range of familiarity. Assume you're awkward when you can't eat for a huge segment of a day. By and by, when you practice 48-hour fasts once consistently, after specific months, you won't be awkward any more extended when you can't eat for an enormous bit of a day.

Action: Purposefully get yourself in an awkward circumstance. Tim Ferriss urges to sit down on the floor transparently. There are much more choices:

- Sleep a night on the floor.

- Ask for a 10% markdown when you demand an espresso.

- Go seven days without espresso.

Add the hold provision to your actions.

We just control our own special thoughts and actions. Everything else isn't under our prompt control. This is the motivation behind why the Stoics regularly added a hold arrangement to their actions.

The thought: You have a goal in mind and put forth a valiant effort to achieve this goal. However, all isn't heavily influenced by you. In this way, you incorporate a spare explanation, for instance, "God willing," "fate allowing," "if nothing balances me" to the action.

Seneca depicted it as seeks after, "I have to do such and such, insofar as nothing occurs, which may show a deterrent to my choice."

This gives you an agreement over whatever the outcome will be. Since you know, it's less heavily influenced by you. A quick individual doesn't mistake his yearnings for how the universe will go.

- "I will voyage over the ocean if nothing balances me."

- "Tomorrow, I will go to the shoreline, fate allowing."

- "You should get my letter by Thursday, God willing."

This requires you give your best for all that is heavily influenced by you, and after that, recognize whatever happens that is not heavily influenced by you. You understand that a definitive outcome is outside your ability to control.

Action: What is something you expect to do; however, the outcome isn't absolutely up to you? Use a similar stipulation. For example, when you go out, tell your mother, "See you later, fate allowing." She won't be content with that, yet it's magnificent preparing for you. Speak Little words, Speak Well, Don't Gossip of anything, and make sure to Listen Instead.

Calm is the Stoic's friend.

Epictetus said we should possibly talk if basic and not about normal spot stuff. "Most importantly, don't snitch about people, adulating, accusing, or looking at them."

It couldn't be any more obvious, enjoying snitch and making a decision about people who care for no situation present is generally not a fair activity.

Moreover, don't yak about yourself. Everybody talks fundamentally about themselves, so you may better tune in and be of help instead of discussing your night out.

Ask yourself, OK, prefer to hear people continuing forever about themselves? No. With the exception of maybe if it's a humorist.

Action: Observe yourself just as others in discussions. Do you see how everybody is attempting to associate what's being said with themselves? Try not to go on and on; endeavor to tune in and bolster others. Cause them to feel better.

- **Test Your Impressions**

How frequently have you reacted naturally to some circumstance just out of your initial presentation?

Basically, consider how regularly people get irritated at various drivers when driving. People swear, show fingers, and get outstandingly irritated at various drivers, just out of feeling. We have the feeling that the other driver is a no brainer and baam, picked. Be that as it may, we don't have the foggiest idea.

Conceivably it was our privilege to drive, yet maybe his child is biting the dust on the front seat; perhaps his vehicle will get snatched rather than our own, potentially he did just not give full thought. Besides, maybe you have accomplished something similar previously. More frequently than nothing out and out horrible has happened.

So peaceful down, take a full breath and restrict the drive to react right away. We would favor not to react rashly to impressions, so ask yourself, "I'm getting perturbed… Does this look good? What decisively happened?"

Epictetus narrates we should ask whether it is up to us or not and if not, by then, we should state, "By then it's none of my anxiety."

There's no explanation in responding sincerely to something we can't deal with. It isn't heavily influenced by us, just our reaction is. So pick the perfect reaction and continue forward. In various cases, the best reaction is no reaction.

Action: Test your initial presentations. In the event that they are unhelpful, by then, pick a progressively intelligent reaction. Potentially you don't need to react using any and all means. As a rule, we react to trifles. This isn't fundamental, and we can expel it.

How Might I Use Virtue Here and Now?

Here's outstanding amongst other Stoic compositions I have encountered up to this point. By Epictetus:

"For each challenge, review the advantages you have inside you to adjust to it. Impelled, by observing an alluring man or a wonderful woman, you will find inside you the opposite force of persistence. It looked with torment; you will find the force of tirelessness. In the event that you are offended, you will find tolerance. In time, you will create to be sure that there is positively not a solitary impression that you won't have the moral method to endure."

Magnificent!

You can use any circumstance, each challenge, as a way to deal with training greatness and improve as an individual. You just need to apply greatness and reason consistently.

The thought is so basic. With everything that happens, you can rehearse honesty. That is the least you can do. That is a safe technique to recognize everything that happens generously in light of the fact that you can take at any rate something extraordinary from it, correctly the demonstration of balance.

You can go well beyond tolerating everything that happens by cherishing everything that happens. That is called 'love fati.' Everything happens explicitly for you. Furthermore, you find the opportunity to value it.

Action: When you face a clumsy circumstance, ask yourself, "What is my best reaction here?" "By what technique would I be able to apply reason and honorableness right now?"

Is this the condition that I so dreaded?

This is a movement from Seneca.

That is the genuine stunt: You set aside a specific number of days when you go with basically nothing and decrepit sustenance, dress in ratty pieces of clothing, and ask yourself whether that is the thing that you so feared.

Then again, experience a late evening dozing on the floor, quick for 24 hours, scour.

We think little things. An agreeable bed. Enough sustenance. Bubbling water. On the off chance that you surrender those things just for two or three days, you will value them all together later. You will welcome them.

The thought is triple. 1. We should value our life more and don't think little of everything. 2. We should not fear losing everything. It will, regardless, be good. We can live with less; it isn't so terrible. We should try to balance it. Guarantee less, be increasingly freed.

Action: Deprive yourself of something quickly, and from that point onward, appreciate the condemnation out of it when you do it once more.

Try not to Be happy with Learning – Practice!

Practice at rehearsing these exercises.

Try not to be fulfilled now since you skimmed over the exercises. You should pick in any event one exercise and start right away. As Epictetus asked well, "On the off chance that you didn't get acquainted with these things in the solicitation to show them eventually, what did you learn them for?"

It couldn't be any more obvious; I don't need to tell you again how to do these exercises – you just need to start.

What is the most terrible that could occur?

When you set out to achieve something, ask yourself, "What is the most horrible that could happen?"

That is exemplary for Stoicism, and it's one of its fundamental thoughts: To prepare for the poo to happen and still have the choice to take it with calm and pick the most splendid possible reaction.

Various people have a sort of plan, and when something occurs, that isn't as indicated by that course of action, they have a conventional old passionate giant out. By and by, this isn't valuable and can be checked.

Just prepare for terrible stuff to happen. The image that your vehicle will break done on your way to the noteworthy imminent representative get together. Additionally, in the event that it happens, you'll have the alternative to take it much better. It will look at the present suck. However, you won't find peculiarity out.

We needn't bother with the most observably awful to happen, yet we should be prepared on the off chance that it happens. On the off chance that you have envisioned an awkward circumstance before it happens, you'll have the alternative to take it much better and stay calmer and right now the choice to make its best.

You possibly get crushed on the off chance that you have not seen that coming…

Action: What do you intend to do in the next days? Picture what could turn out seriously and choose a snappy reaction. Imagine a scenario where… by then, I will.

- **Have a good example in mind**

The Stoics used the Stoic Sage is a genuine model.

The Sage is a theoretical great; he is the ideal extraordinary and clever person.

Directly, don't pressure; you will never be impeccable in that sense. Likewise, you shouldn't be. Regardless, it's been shown to be significant to have an individual in mind we have to interest or copy. It's not about the impersonation since you are uncommon and should put forth an attempt not to resemble another person. We can pick up from others.

In distressing circumstances, ask yourself:

- "What may the Sage do?"

- "What may the ideal daddy do?"
- "What may LeBron James do?"
- "What may Batman do?"

If you have some genuine model in mind, fantastic! Envision that he is watching and watching you, and you should be as high as possible. This phenomenal model game isn't commonly about the genuine models yet about carrying mindfulness into the circumstance. Since significant inside yourself, you appreciate what's the best activity.

Action: Bring mindfulness into normal circumstances and ask what your genuine model would do. Or, on the other hand, ask what the ideal dad, mum, kin, partner, companion, darling, sportsman would do.

- **Love Fati – Love your Fate**

The Stoics endeavored to concentrate on what they can control. In addition, fate wasn't one of them.

So they urged not to need for reality to be any unique and rather recognize and value it for what it's worth. They regularly used the "dog restricted to a moving truck" purposeful anecdote:

The adroit man resembles a pooch chained to a moving truck, running merrily close by and productively keeping pace with it, though an imbecile resembles a canine that grumbly fights against the rope yet winds up pulled nearby the truck at any rate.

We can't change what comes to pass throughout everyday life. So the most intelligent thing is to recognize as opposed to fighting each barely noticeable detail that unfolds. We're similar to that pooch restricted to a truck: we're just as free as the length of the chain. Accordingly, we preferably welcome the experience over getting pulled along.

To hate what happens is to expect you have a choice in that issue wrongly.

Action: When something comes to pass, ask yourself whether you can do what needs to be done or not. If not, if it's not under your yet under fate's influence, by then, recognize it all things considered. There's no sense in battling with this present reality; it'll just make you miserable.

- Nonresistance: Don't need for reality to be any not the same as it is.

- Nonjudgmental: Don't condemn events; simply recognize them as they seem to be.

- Nonattachment: Things go to and fro; don't get excessively appended to what you like.

- **Agony and Sickness – Opportunities for Virtue**

Stoic teacher Epictetus was frail. He picked this was a snag to the leg, not to the mind.

The comparable is legitimate for physical torment and contamination. The agony is to the body, not the mind. We can pick what we do with the torment. It is conceivable that we can take a cerebral torment courageously, or we can whimper and whine about it. The choice is up to us.

This movement is about not being taken over by weakness and self-centeredness when we suffer torment. Such liberal reactions will just intensify the circumstance.

Action: Next time you feel a kind of torment endeavor to prepare your exemplary nature and keep it together. Remember, the agony is to the body, not the mind.

- Headache? It's an opportunity to prepare quality.

- Fever? Give your body some rest, no motivation to gripe.

- Choose not to be affected by torment, spare your quietness.

Envision Everything as acquired from fortune

All we truly guarantee is our mind. Everything else can be expelled at a snap.

Your assets, your body, your family, your allies, everything could be evacuated in a second. As per the Stoics, we should value these things as long as we have them, yet not get too appended in light of the fact that they could be gone quickly. Consider everything procured – from nature, fortune, God, or whatever you need – and you can just use it by chance. It might be expelled at a snap. Difficulties and gone. Without prior observation. Without inquiring.

Seneca pondered, in what manner may we see such a lot of hardship occurring on the planet and not envision it occurring with us? It's deadness.

Action: Remind yourself that all that you think to have isn't really yours. Whether or not you paid for it. On the off chance that it will, in general, be expelled at a snap, it's not truly yours.

- Be mindful that all that you hold truly can be expelled without before observe.

- What's your favorite you "have?" Remember, it could be passed by tomorrow.

- Next time you kiss your loved one's goodbye, envision it's the last time.

Remember your Good fortune.

The Stoics were minimalists.

They needed to esteem what they had as opposed to aching for what they didn't have. They were appreciative of what they had throughout everyday life. They endeavored to require whatever they recently had as opposed to wanting things they didn't have.

Essentially, (1) they endeavored to fight their craving to accumulate and swarm stuff. They (2) were appreciative of what they recently had without (3) getting excessively connected to those things.

Action: How much would you need the things you have on the off chance that you didn't have them? Like with various exercises, you can record things. For example, record three things you're thankful for.

- Don't buy the stuff you don't require.

- Appreciate the things you starting at now have.

- Don't get excessively appended to these things you're appreciative for.

Excuse the wrongs of others.

The Stoics accepted that everybody endeavors to do what he believes is right. Whether or not it's obviously not.

People don't mess up purposefully; they go about as they might suspect is right. Likewise, we should feel frustrated about as opposed to blaming them.

In what manner may we loathe somebody when we understand he didn't have the foggiest idea about any better? Right, we should be tolerant and kind. We have to excuse the wrongs of others, as Jesus expressed, "Father, pardon them, for they don't fathom what they are doing."

Action: Before you explode at somebody, uncover to yourself that she didn't have the foggiest idea about any better. However, you do, and accordingly, you can be thoughtful and pardoning.

• Don't search for retaliation when somebody wrongs you – mean from deficiency. Be tolerant and kind.

• Pity as opposed to blaming transgressors – they are blinded in their most necessary resource: their mind.

• If somebody is mean to you, by then, endeavor to believe it to prepare. We're all learning and attempting to give indications of progress, scratches happen. So shake it off and continue forward, it's happened distinctly in preparing.

Purchase Tranquility Instead

This is an immaterial virtuoso.

One of the primary goals of the Stoics was to have the choice to stay calm even regardless of setback. Whatever a Stoic faces, he needs to stay peaceful and sensible.

Frequently when something occurs, I don't care for, and which mixes this inward ire and vitality, I let myself know, "I buy quietness." And continue ahead calmly. In reality, even with a smile.

This announcement alone justified all of the books I read on Stoicism. I significantly ask you to endeavor to fuse these words into your Stoic way of life. Trust me; it'll be supported, in spite of all the difficulty.

The main admonition: It requires enough regard for step in the middle of the improvement and reaction. In the event that you deal with that, you'll quickly benefit altogether from these words.

Action: Bring mindfulness into your life, and at whatever point something is stimulating shock and uneasiness inside you, let yourself know, "I buy peacefulness."

- When you spill some wine over your articles of clothing – buy tranquility.
- When your roomie doesn't do the dishes – buy tranquility.
- When your favored games bunch yields a late equalizer – buy tranquility.

It is far simpler to look at something fairly and to keep up the balance when little burdens, or even calamities, come to pass as opposed to ourselves.

Be that as it may, why? What makes us imagine that we are the universe's phenomenal dear that is significantly huger than others?

Wouldn't it be better If we could react similarly when something loads us? We are not extraordinary. What unfolded has happened to various people previously and will happen to various later on.

The universe doesn't treat us any uniquely in contrast to other people; it isn't after us. Things unfold in the average solicitation of things. Realizing this can give us comfort.

Action: When something "awful" in any case, what happens. In the event that you are lamented about something, endeavor this movement.

We frequently get an unnecessary issue in light of our creative minds. We mess up and overlook this isn't such a noteworthy thing that appeared differently in relation to for as far back as we can recollect. We revolve around something and think this is gigantically huge, yet it is never as critical as it shows up while we are contemplating it.

That is when the point of view can be truly valuable. Take the view from above. Envision you're up in the sky and believe yourself to be a modest bit in a little house, in a little city, in a still little country appeared differently in relation to the whole planet. Furthermore, the whole planet is small stood out from the universe.

Your issues can't be such a critical thing in the impressive subject of your life. From above, things seem, by all accounts, to be logically trifling, which urges you to see it with detachment.

What's more, that everything is short-lived. Look at what issues single people are worried about.

John has a headache and is particularly worried about this. On the contrary piece of the course of action, people are continued running over by a Tsunami, and in one more spot, people get into bomb blasts.

That cerebral torment looks like a joke from above. Like most various issues we worry about.

Action: Imagine leaving your body and ascending higher upwards the sky and looking down on yourself and the things around you. Go perpetually raised and look at your city, your country, your landmass, ultimately our planet. The audit that your body lives down there…

HELPFUL STOIC EXERCISE

Distinctive Stoic exercises that you can do to develop a Stoic perspective. While this is significant for the possible Stoic, I feel that everyone can benefit from these exercises. In the event that you don't ponder Stoicism, by then, here would be a good beginning, or you can examine a few various papers I've made, and you should quickly understand the general thought.

This isn't some extraordinary ballyhoo; any person who acknowledges me realizes that I object to the whole thought of "powerful nature." These exercises have been used by countless people since they work, taking everything into account, not in some nonexistent far away land. They are rational, and they don't require any equipment, with the exception of a working mind.

These exercises have been around for an enormous number of years, and the clarification that they are up 'til now appropriate today is on the grounds that they are grounded incomparable way experience and in like way sense.

EXERCISE #1: EARLY MORNING REFLECTION

It doesn't take a logical virtuoso to comprehend this one. You need to reflect, speedily close to the start of the day. It's, in actuality, more nuanced than that. It's not just about masterminding what you will do that day, and it's about how you may respond to what you will do and besides what others will do.

Stick like there's no tomorrow to the going with standard: Not to respect trouble, never to trust in progress, and consistently to take full note of fortune's penchant for continuing comparably anyway she sees fit, her as if she were truly going to do all that it is in her impact to do. Whatever you have been expecting for a long time comes as to a lesser degree a shock.— Seneca

At first, be grateful that you have woken up, various people won't have this advantage today.

Additionally, plan how you will get a handle on your excellencies and avoid your obscenities. Pick a particular philosophical resolution or an individual quality you have to create and consider how you can go along with it into the day ahead. Soundly check how you will deal with any irksome conditions that know may well develop.

Thirdly, prompt yourself that the principle things you can control are your contemplations and your exercises. Everything else is wild.

Errand;

1. In the event that you find a workable pace and have time, go out for a walk and welcome the rising sun while ruminating over making yourself as a person.

2. Perform light exercises using your own one of a kind bodyweight. Consider your own one of kind mortality and the manner in which that you will age.

EXERCISE #2: A VIEW FROM ABOVE

This exercise is proposed to remind you about how little you for sure are, and how little noteworthiness most things are. So to speak, to give you a sentiment of the all-inclusive strategy.

It's direct, and you use your innovative mind to endeavor to relate yourself to the whole world and past.

Two different ways to move toward this:

1. Follow a guided reflection.

2. Do it without anyone else's help. This is my supported technique, as you don't require any equipment. It will, in general, be done wherever. I recommend taking off to somewhere extricating up. Unmistakably I can tell you unequivocally what to imagine since I'm not you, yet I would recommend starting over the fogs and a while later step by step come closer to the world and the people in it. Try not to spare a moment to start a mess progressively removed away in some distant spot of the universe. Watch everything going on: first kisses, wars, exposures, learning, marvelous appearances, blocked driving conditions, and whatever else you can imagine. Watch, nonetheless, don't condemn. By and by view yourself as in association with most of this. Realize that an enormous number of the things you hold to be noteworthy are simply commonly significant. Understand that you are just modestly considerable.

Extra Assignments

1. Take a stab at setting time as you do this exercise. Imagine yourself walking around urban networks, and everything is amazingly still. See that precise moment.

2. Endeavor this exercise; be that as it may, in a substitute period. This can truly hammer home the manner in which that you once didn't exist and over the long haul.

EXERCISE #3: CONTEMPLATION OF THE MAN (OR WOMAN) DESIRE

This exercise is proposed to give an impulse to change towards transforming into an ideal individual. This is a perpetual strategy.

Consider the attributes which make up the ideal person. For the prosperity of straightforwardness, we ought to expect that the Greek and Roman statues address the physical flawlessness and focus on the psychological edges.

What qualities make up the ideal character? In specific respects, this is a genuine problematic request to answer, and perhaps it is easier to concentrate on what may an ideal individual do in some irregular condition. From the exercises of this ideal individual, we would then have the option to endeavor to choose their inside attributes and, preferably, begin to duplicate them. Review that the ideal individual doesn't exist…

Extra Assignments

1. Make an overview of real genuine models, past or present, and research what makes them great. Find the best attributes of these individuals and discard any negative character deserts.

2. You can moreover plan something opposite for looking at the ideal man. Inspect the most exceedingly awful kind of individual conceivable and try to refrain from being that way.

EXERCISE #4: CULTIVATING PHILANTHROPY

For a certain something, we ought to portray unselfishness:

The craving to propel the welfare of others.

Contrary to display day figuring, money isn't the ideal approach to transform into a philanthropic person. For sure, anyone can transform into a contributor, and it just requires the right outlook towards others.

The issue is that as an issue, obviously, we will all in all life as if we were being encased in a movement of circles, one inside the other, many equivalents to a Russian doll. Each hover addresses a consistently higher great way from our genuine selves.

So how might we create good cause? Our goal should be to endeavor to bring everyone into a shut circle. So consider your family an increase of yourself and your related inhabitants as your family, right to looking at humankind as a whole as country individuals. The Stoic intellectual Hierocles even went the degree that cliché that we should consider our to be just as they were parts of our own body, like an arm or a leg.

This requires a huge move in setting and a lot of effort; in any case, it has its central focuses:

• You end up not become too much associated with any single individual who leaves you less revealed

• A greater companion organizes, which implies a more noteworthy introduction to different social orders and viewpoints. This is an incredibly open entryway for learning.

Errands

1. Strike up an enchanting conversation with an untouchable.

2. Let your dear sidekicks understand that you consider them an element of your family and that they should have the alternative to rely upon all of you things considered.

EXERCISE #5: SELF RETREAT

While there are various legitimate supports to dare to the most distant corners of the planet, doing thusly to find concordance or opportunity isn't one of them. It's very unphilosophical. Huge quietness and opportunity are things that began from inside, so in the event that you are escaping from the scholarly dissension, you are escaping from yourself. Disastrously when you make an outing, you have to bring yourself along for the journey.

Allow me to offer you a less perplexing and besides much more affordable approach to find critical quietness and opportunity with this exercise. Routinely travel inside your mind, particularly in case you need critical tolerance or opportunity. No spot else is anyone as apparently. You can be variously suitable here, at present. All that is expected of you is five to ten minutes consistently to finish off the world and to take into consideration your own one of a kind mind.

People search for withdraws for themselves in the farmland by the seashore, in the inclines, and you likewise have made it your affinity to hurt for that little paying mind to whatever else. Regardless, this is all around unphilosophical, when it is possible for you to withdraw into yourself at whatever point you please; for no spot would one have the option to withdraw into more prominent agreement or opportunity from thought than inside one's own soul, especially when an individual incorporates such things inside him that he simply needs to see them recover from that moment perfect effortlessness of cerebrum (and by straightforwardness of mind I add up to nothing other than having one's mind in extraordinary solicitation). So consistently grant yourself this retreat, consequently energize yourself, yet keep inside you compact and fundamental resolutions that will be adequate, from the beginning experience, to scour you from all agony.

I starting late saw a video about a prisoner who understood that he would spend a mind-blowing rest in disengagement. He discussed how he could, regardless, escape from the four dividers of his cell by examining and thinking. This makes you wonder what being a prisoner suggests, and if there are a couple of ways we are by and large prisoners in different sorts of correctional facilities. The person who is truly permitted to do what he appreciates may be sanely caught in wretchedness or progressively horrible.

Two or three things you may need to think about when on a self retreat:

• You are not aggravated by events yet by your evaluation of events.

• Everything is continually giving indications of progress, and there is no way around it.

• You won't live until the finish of time.

Undertaking;

1. Attempt and practice self retreat in non-immaculate conditions. You could try doing it in a comparable room as someone sitting before the TV or perhaps on a journey in an open vehicle.

2. Visit Calm.com to empower you to loosen up before starting in case you are encountering issues when you first give this a shot.

EXERCISE 6: THE PHILOSOPHICAL JOURNAL

The qualification here is that rather than clarifying just on what has happened in your life before, you analyze it from a Stoical perspective. You can use a philosophical journal as an instrument to locate your own one of a kind lacks and to follow the manner in which you change after some time. By steady reflection, we can improve our present and future life.

By organizing your future exercises according to an ethical framework and after that later, you can recollect and see what prerequisites to change reliant on what happened. This Stoic exercise is definitely not hard to unite with a common dairy, and on the off chance that you do it right, unavoidably, there should be no qualification between a "conventional" journal area and a philosophical one.

Assignments;

1. Keep a regular philosophical journal for one month.

2. Peruse the philosophical journal called "Examinations" of the Roman head and realist Marcus Aurelius.

EXERCISE #7: THE STRIPPING METHOD

The derivation behind this exercise is that every situation has various layers, many equivalents to an onion. Each layer addresses something that we bring to the situation and not just the condition. It's simply by considering the inside issues without the decently immaterial layers we incorporate that we can go about according to a good authentic structure. Stop considering your reputation or whatever individual piece of the room you figure you may get as a significant part of the condition when working out what to do in a given situation. Ask yourself the going with requests:

- What worth does this situation bring to everyone? You might be amazed at how regularly the fitting reaction is "none."
- What kind of attributes does this situation require? If you have these qualities, by then extraordinary, in case not, by then, consider this condition a good chance to make them.

At the point when we are growing up, an impressive parcel of us fight to pick what we have to do in our lives, in case we strip this request down significantly, it's connected to finding something fulfilling and essential to advance toward. From the outset, it justifies neglecting the issue of adjustment or others' longing for what you should do else you may end up continuing with an actual existence which is far ousted from who you truly are.

I really struggled with this growing up. I had an astounding start in life to the extent of guidance at a top school, I had lived in various spots, and I had a strong melodic youth. I got every open door available, yet I was in such frenzy about what I would do in my life, that I quit school before

I finished and never anytime set off for college. While I wouldn't recommend along these lines to everyone, it, at last, turned out very well for me.

Assignment;

1. Ask yourself the going with a request: What may I do if money was not an issue?

2. Answer the over the request, and from that point forward, continue to do just that.

EXERCISE #8: BEDTIME REFLECTION

This is the opposite side of exercise number one, Early Morning Reflection. This time, instead of contemplating what will happen, you consider what has happened. Normally replay your entire day and a short time later asks yourself the going with requests:

• Did I carry on as shown by all accounts?

• Did I relate with people with whom I teamed up inside a very much arranged and attentive way?

• What obscenities have I combated?

• Have I made myself an unrivaled individual by building up my standards?

There is nothing ending you preparing for the next day. Try not to stop for a second to record two or three notes on interesting points around the start of the day. This all associations up with the next day's Early Morning Reflection.

Figuratively speaking: Learn from your slip-ups.

Undertakings

1. Record one thing you have to improve the next day, paying little heed to pretty much nothing. You will be amazed at how you change in case you keep this up for an impressive time span.

2. B that this day has finished, and there is nothing you would now have the option to do to change it. Recognize everything that has happened, whether or not positive or negative.

EXERCISE #9: NEGATIVE VISUALIZATION

I have oftentimes seen how the wonder of Hedonic Adaptation suggests that we constantly become accustomed to the things we have, and a short time later begins to disparage them. The negative recognition is a fundamental exercise that can remind us how blessed we are. The explanation is clear, imagine that dreadful things have happened, or that helpful things have not. You pick the size of the disaster:

• Losing all of your advantages

• Never having met your life accomplice.

• Losing a family member

• Losing a sense, for instance, your sight or your hearing.

You can, in like manner, imagine how conditions that you are going to forget about it will turn severely.

While you may envision that this kind of pessimism isn't helpful for a happy and fulfilling life, it can change your life into unadulterated gold by making you comprehend that all these awful things have not happened.

Extra Assignments

1. Attempt and imagine fiascoes happening in the very showing that you wille do. I don't endorse this to everyone, as it isn't for the fearful.

2. Envision having been considered eventually beforehand and all of the things that you would miss since they would not have been structured now.

EXERCISE #10: PHYSICAL SELF-CONTROL TRAINING

This exercise includes in purposefully experiencing physical hardships, and besides forsaking things, one increases in value. To a great extent, one could consider this a practical type of negative recognition.

Physical Self-Control Training fills a twofold need:

• To set ourselves up in the event that we have to go up against physical hardships or we lose a couple, or all, of what we have.

• To prepare ourselves not to need things that are outside of our control. Remember that we can control our thoughts and our exercises.

Remember that you ought to understand everything in life uninhibitedly, many equivalents to sand. You don't hold sand immovably, and else it escapes from your grasp.

Stoic Meditation Exercises

Here are the four Stoic meditation methods it incorporates:

Examination of the Sage.

Envision the instance of the ideal Stoic savvy man or woman, and how they would adjust to various challenges throughout everyday life. Endeavor to verbalize their frames of mind, which you can recollect as short maxims or adages. In like manner, think about models, for instance, Socrates, Zeno, Epictetus, or Marcus Aurelius or other explicit genuine models from history, fiction, or your own life.

Examination of Death.

Intermittently think about your own mortality, seeing it impartially, and as both regular and inescapable. Each morning remind yourself that the day ahead could be your last; each night envisions seeing the day behind you as though it were your last. Endeavor to live grounded in the present moment, valuing the endowment of life as though you're a guest at a festival or supper, which you know will keep going for a short timeframe.

Thought of the Whole.

Envision the whole world as though observed from high above, similar to the celestial creatures looking down from Mount Olympus. On the other hand, endeavor to envision the whole of the real world and your place inside things. Consider additionally, the short existence of each and every material thing, and the short time span that human life keeps going.

Premeditation of Adversity

Work on envisioning diverse "disasters" that could happen upon you, as though they're going on now, while keeping up Stoic objectivity and apathy toward them, concentrating on the qualification between what is up to you and what isn't, and permitting sufficient time for your underlying emotions to decrease normally. Think about how, as a Stoic sage would react to comparable events.

CONCLUSION

In the exceptionally least, you can ask yourself, would you say you are living an acceptable life? In advanced life, there is most likely a ton of us who don't consistently pose this inquiry. What's more, in the event that we have thought about it, our answers may originate from taking a gander at big names or the rich, which eventually causes us to feel desirous. We think they carry on with a decent life since they have loads of cash or can do what they need, or we wish that we were as effective as they were in what we do. In any case, this is misinformed; individuals can have a lousy life regardless of bringing home the bacon.

For certain individuals, the easy street might be as straightforward as bringing up their kids to become upbeat and prosperous grown-ups. Like bringing home the bacon, you can have a lousy life regardless of having fruitful youngsters. Likewise, numerous individuals decide not to have kids or raise a family which this would not apply to.

Numerous searches for the responses to the easy street from lessons from their congregation, mosque, or synagogue. Be that as it may, numerous religions show others what to do to have a decent "the hereafter," not concentrating on what you can do to carry on with a decent life now.

What huge numbers of us don't do is go scanning for these answers by visiting the nearby college's philosophy office. In the passages of a stuffy bundle of scholastics, perhaps a couple of educators who can inform you concerning a part of philosophy that has shown the ways for "easy street" for two or three thousand years. That part of philosophy is called stoic philosophy.

There are numerous other stoic bits of knowledge worth referencing, and the act of stoicism requests that you handle them completely on the off chance that you ever need to start to apply them in your life.

Stoics' contemplated easy street is living with goodness, with self-control and resistance by serving your individual man and lady, and to bring internal tranquility into your life. How the Stoics trained their understudies to accomplish this is entrancing, and huge numbers of you may discover astonishing. So for my next post, I will dive into the subtleties on how somebody can apply the stoic practices into day by day life to accomplish righteousness and euphoria with the goal which you can carry on with a decent life.

CPSIA information can be obtained
at www.ICGtesting.com
Printed in the USA
LVHW061936250521
688445LV00009B/900

9 781008 952416